GUNZ N HOZEZ AIRBRUSH

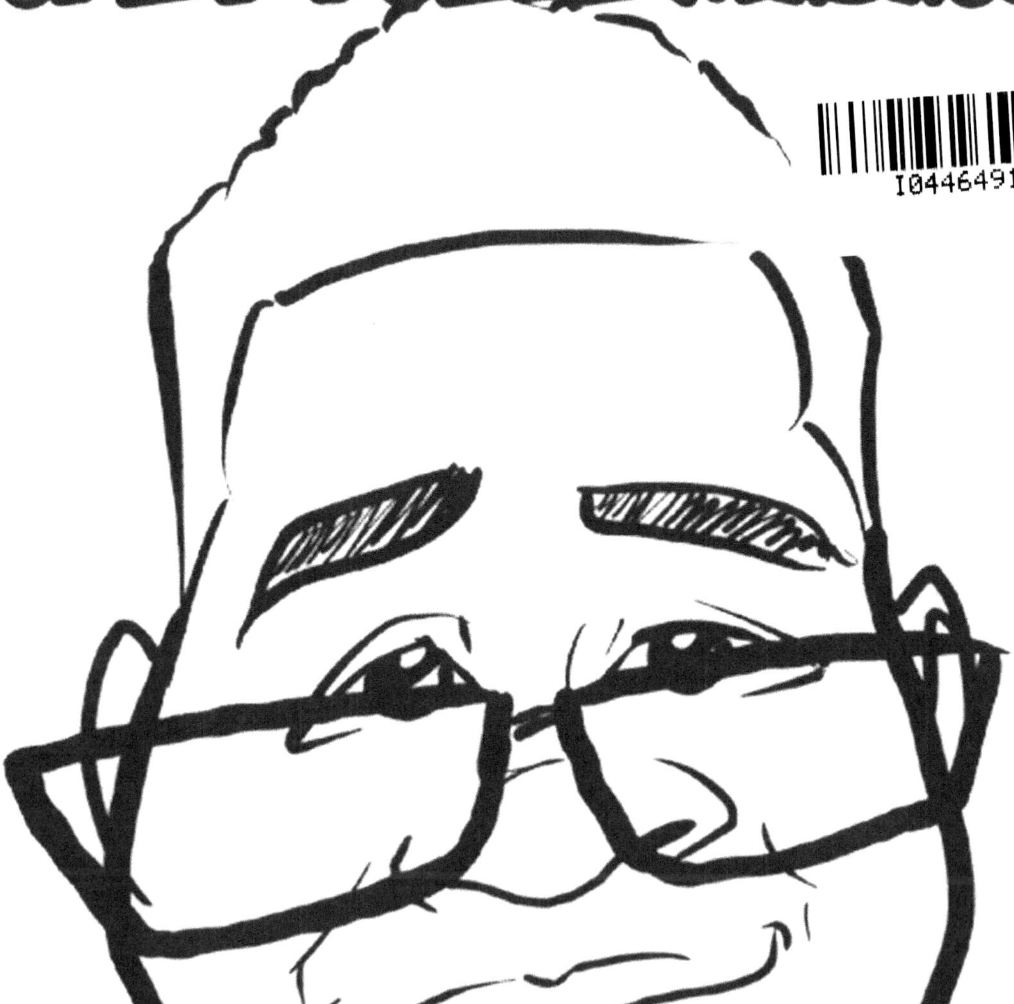

CHRISTOPHER RILEY

HONK ENTERTAINMENT

REY_CANALES

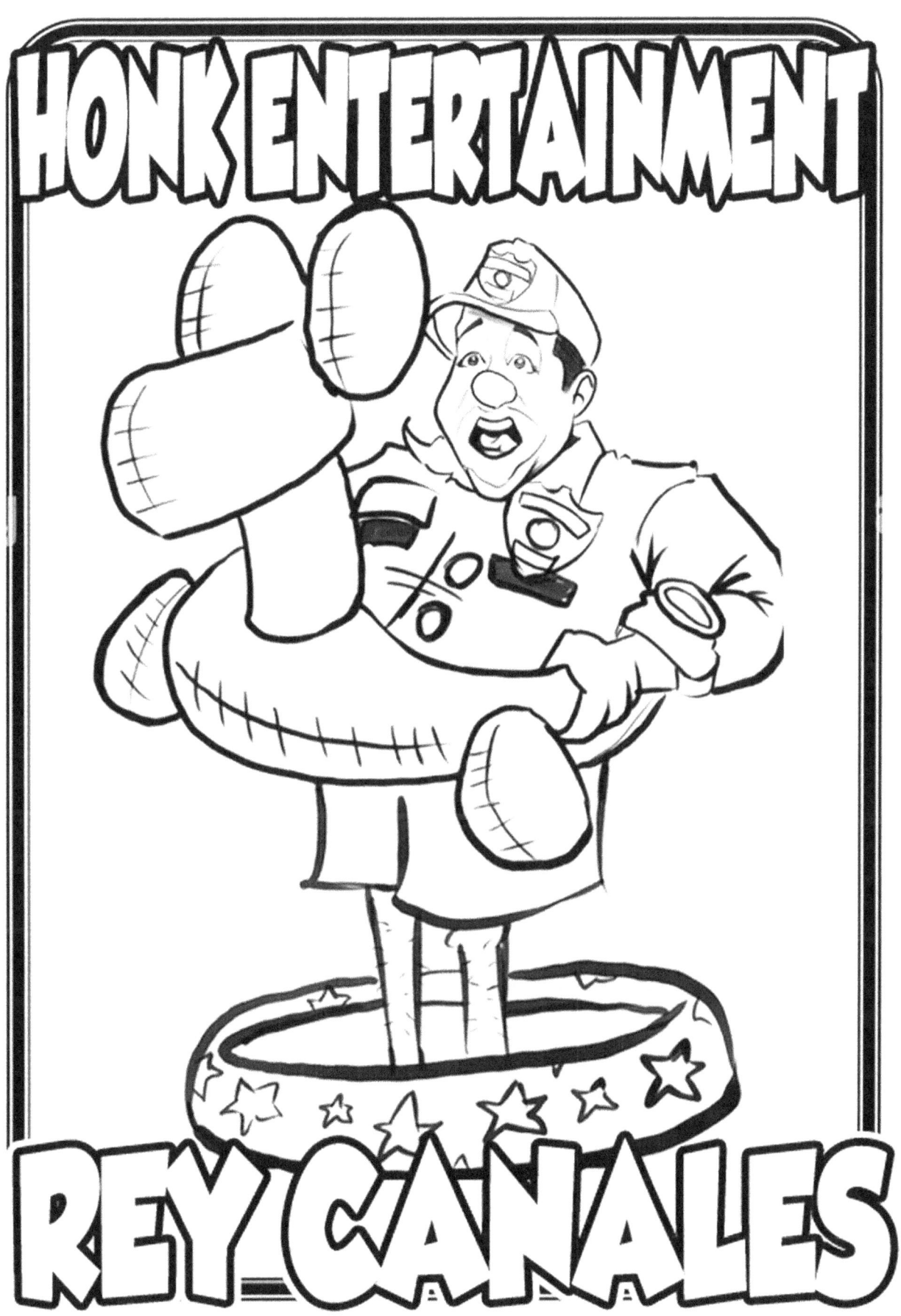

WCA-BIG AIRBRUSH

PAT GAINES

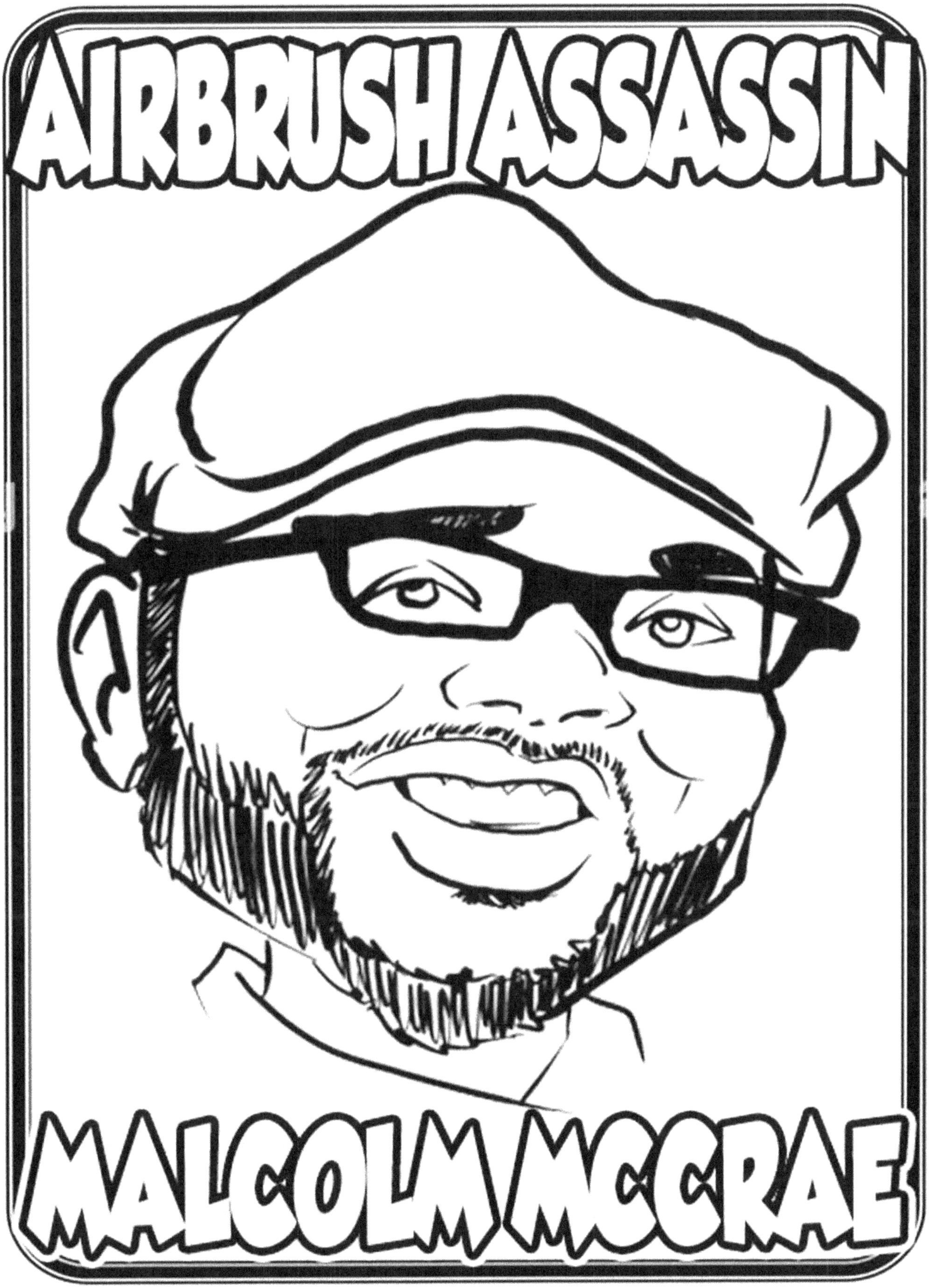
AIRBRUSH ASSASSIN
MALCOLM MCCRAE

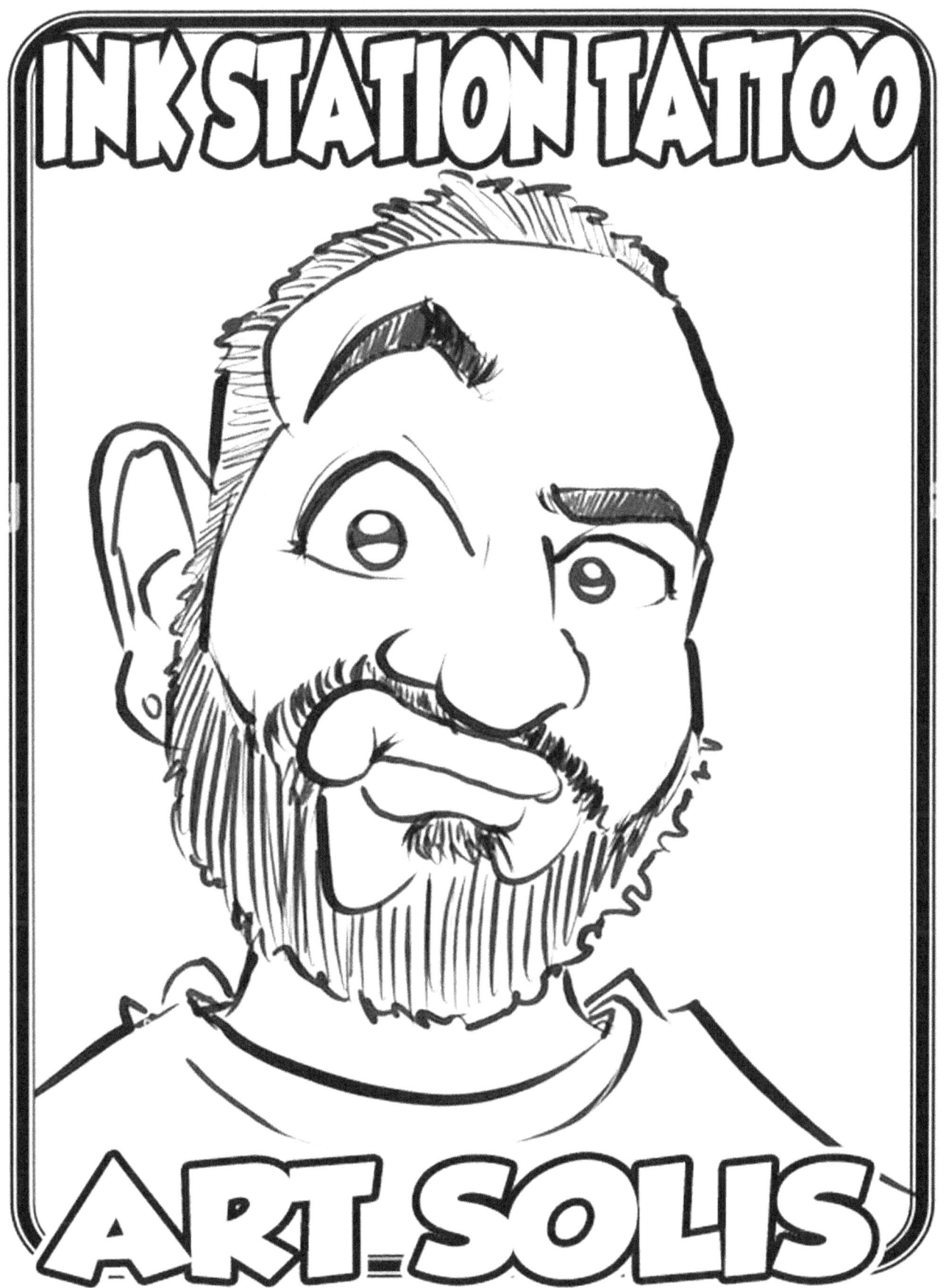

AIRBRUSH LIBRARIAN

BECKY TOWNSEND

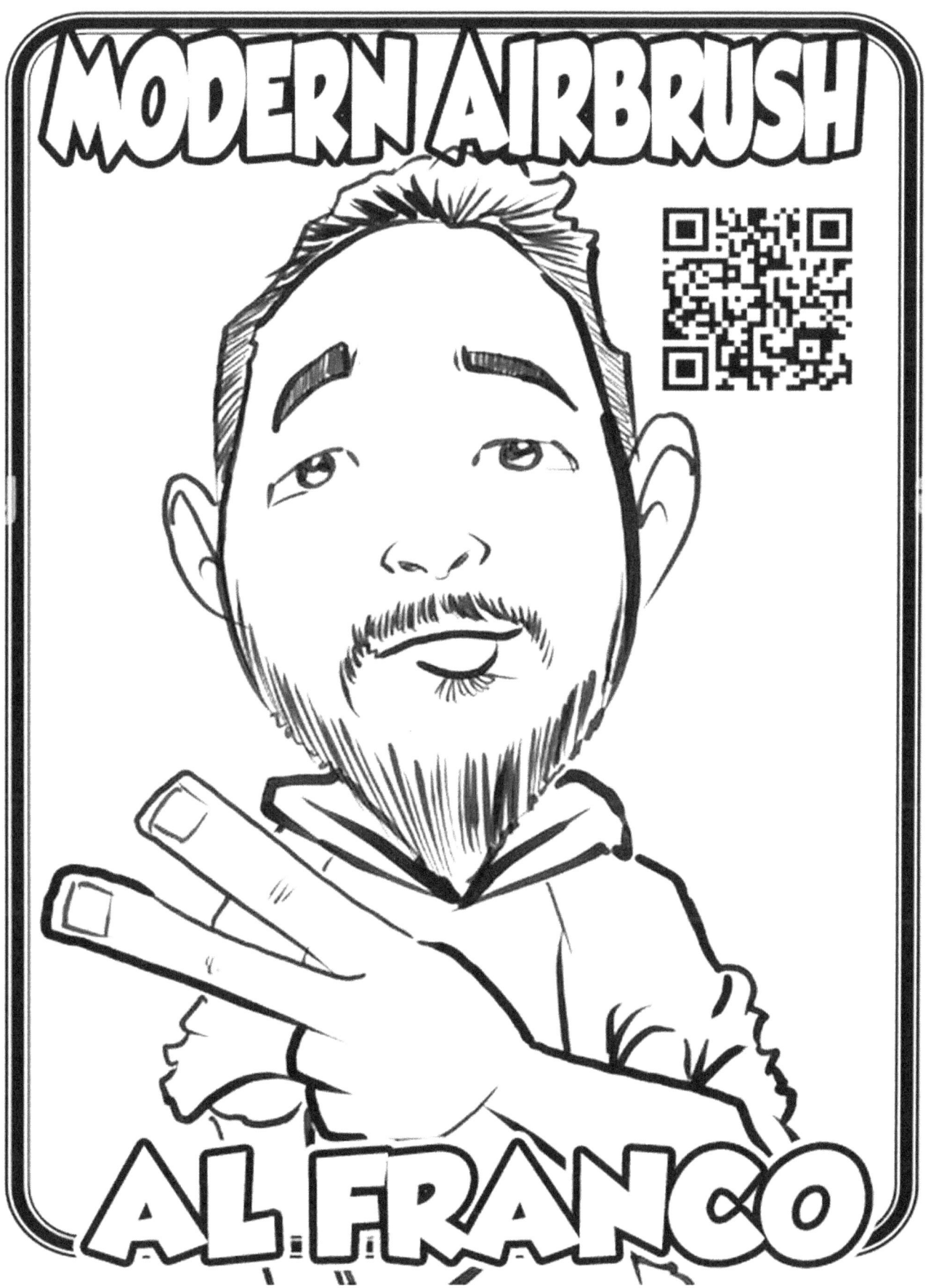

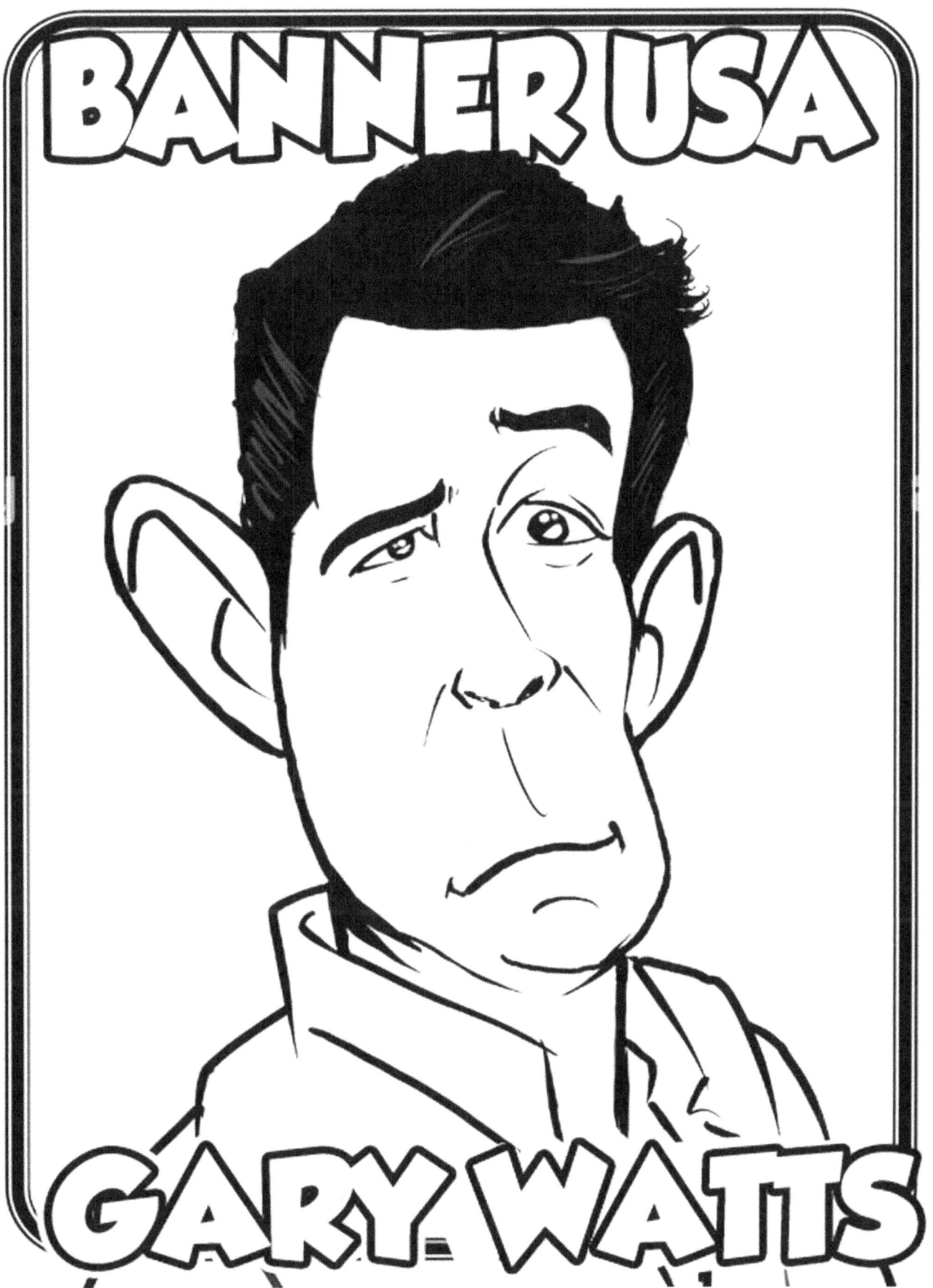

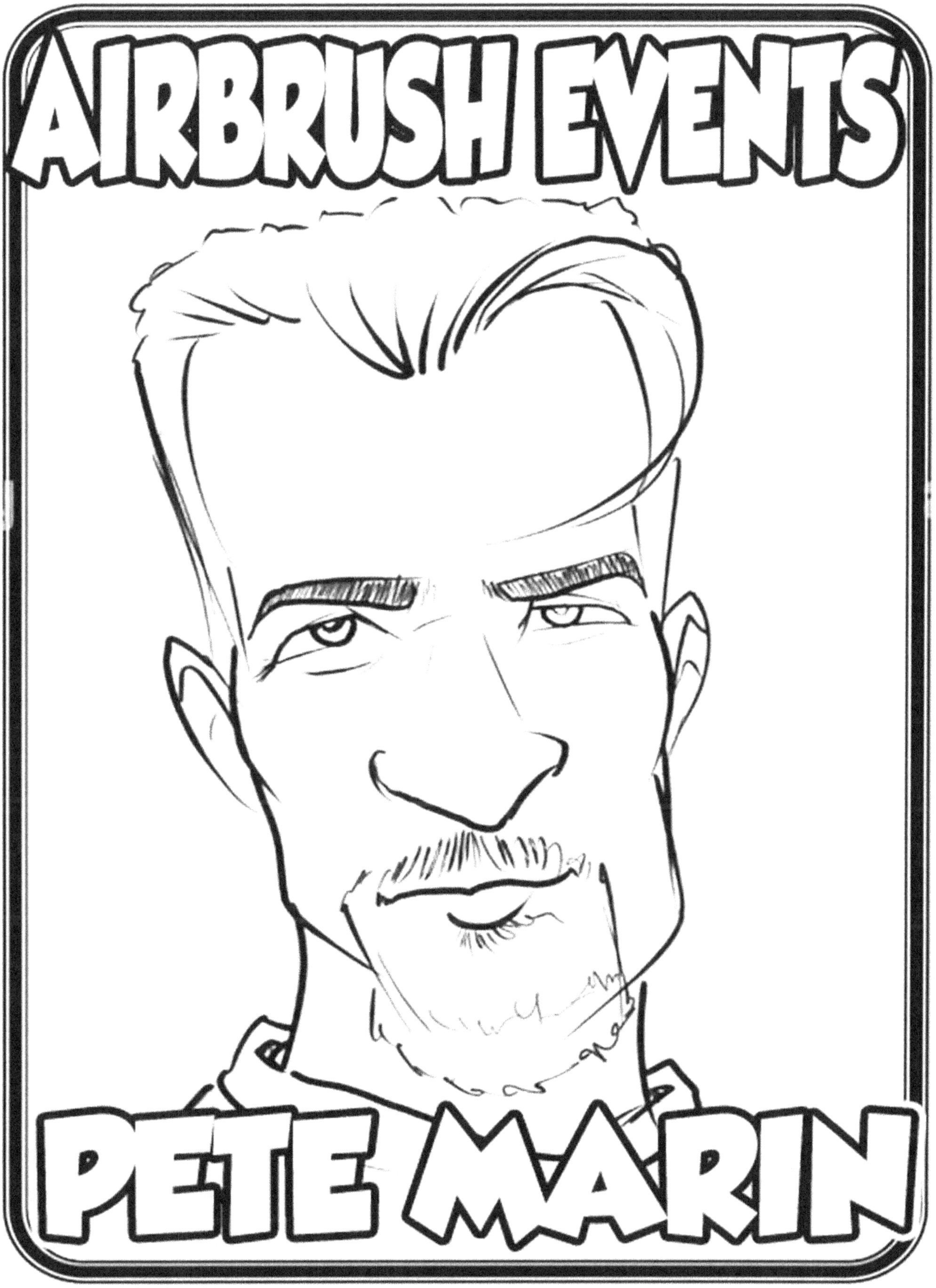
AIRBRUSH EVENTS
PETE MARIN

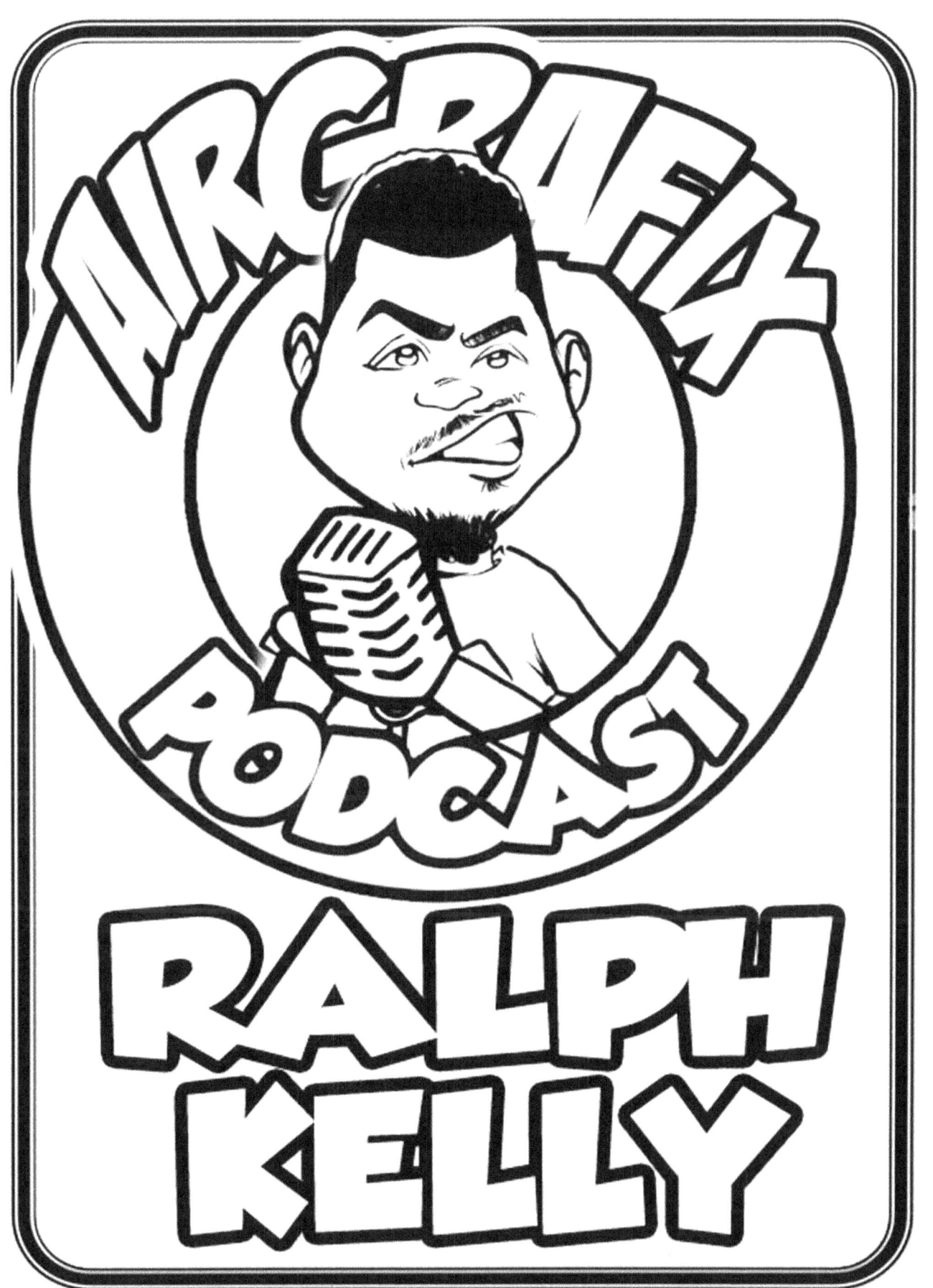

AIRBRUSH HOF

TOM DAVIDSON

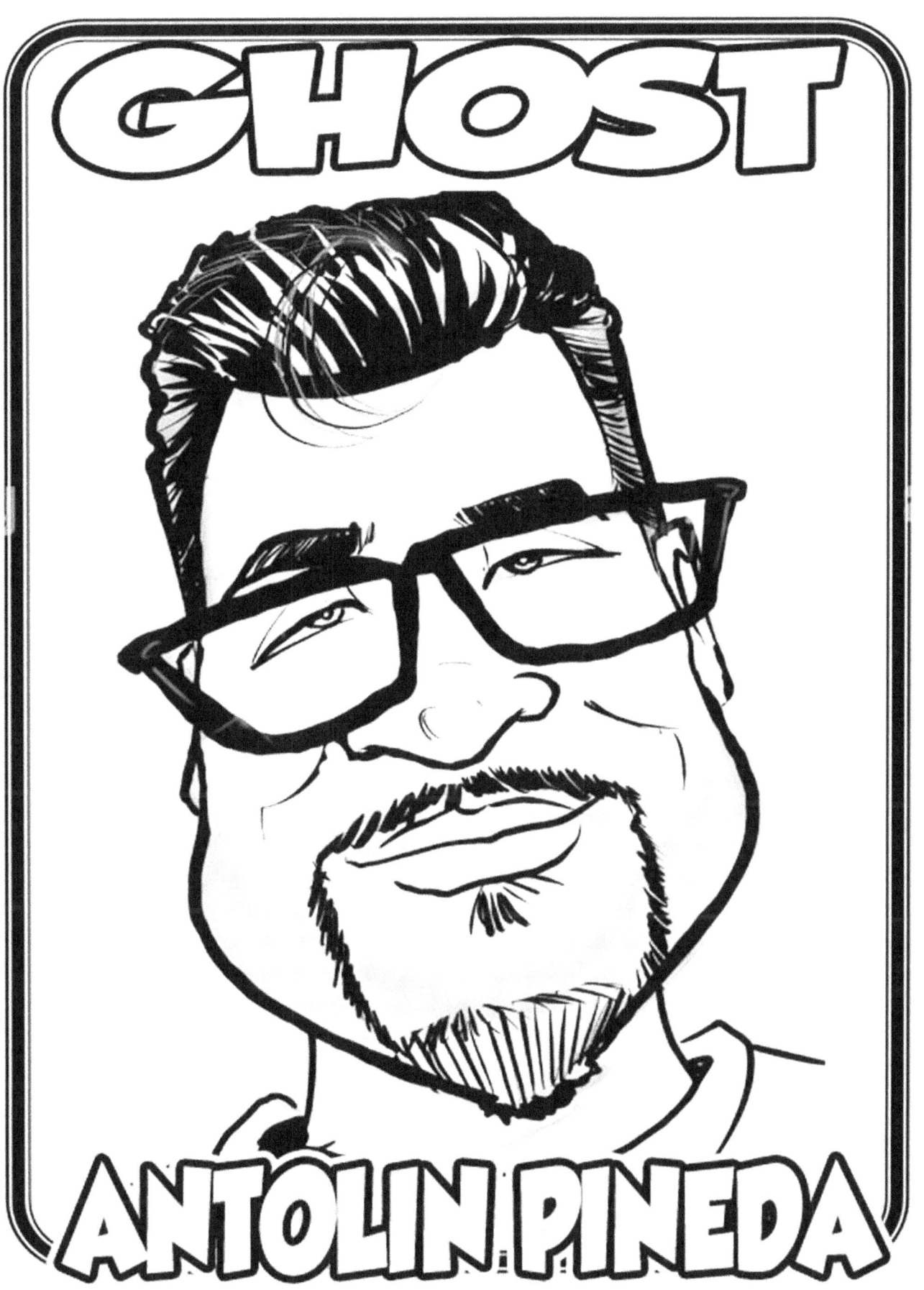

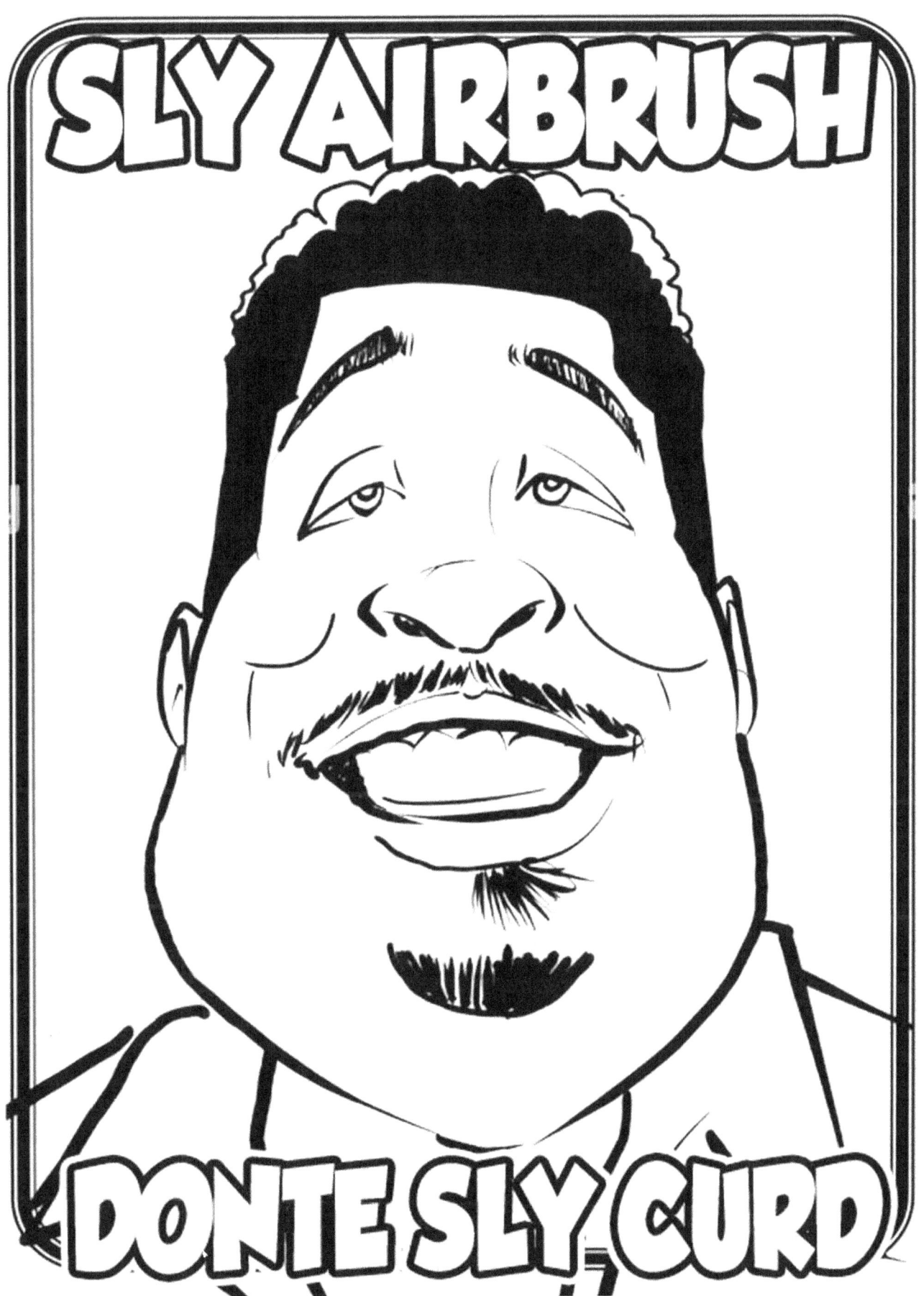

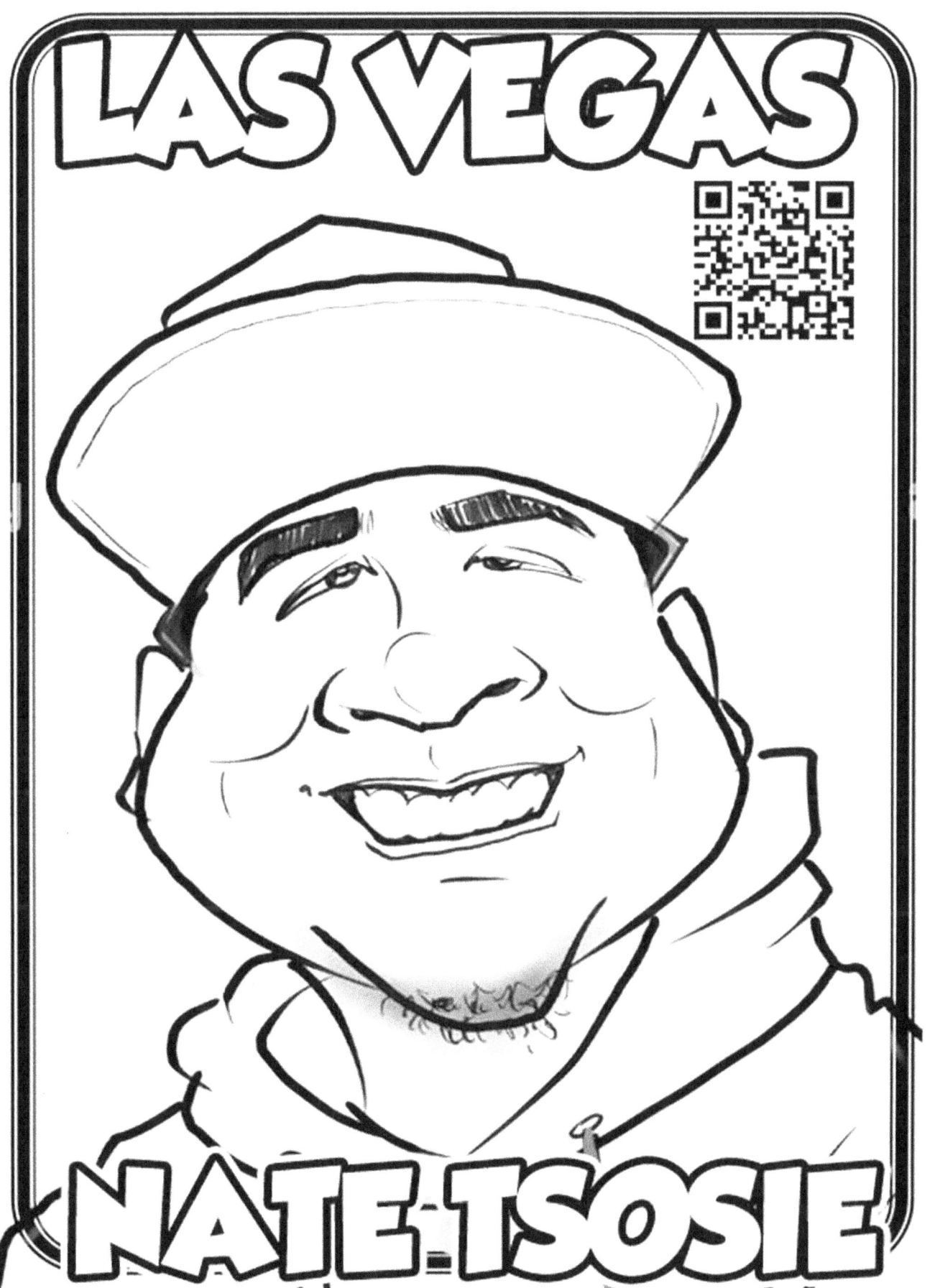

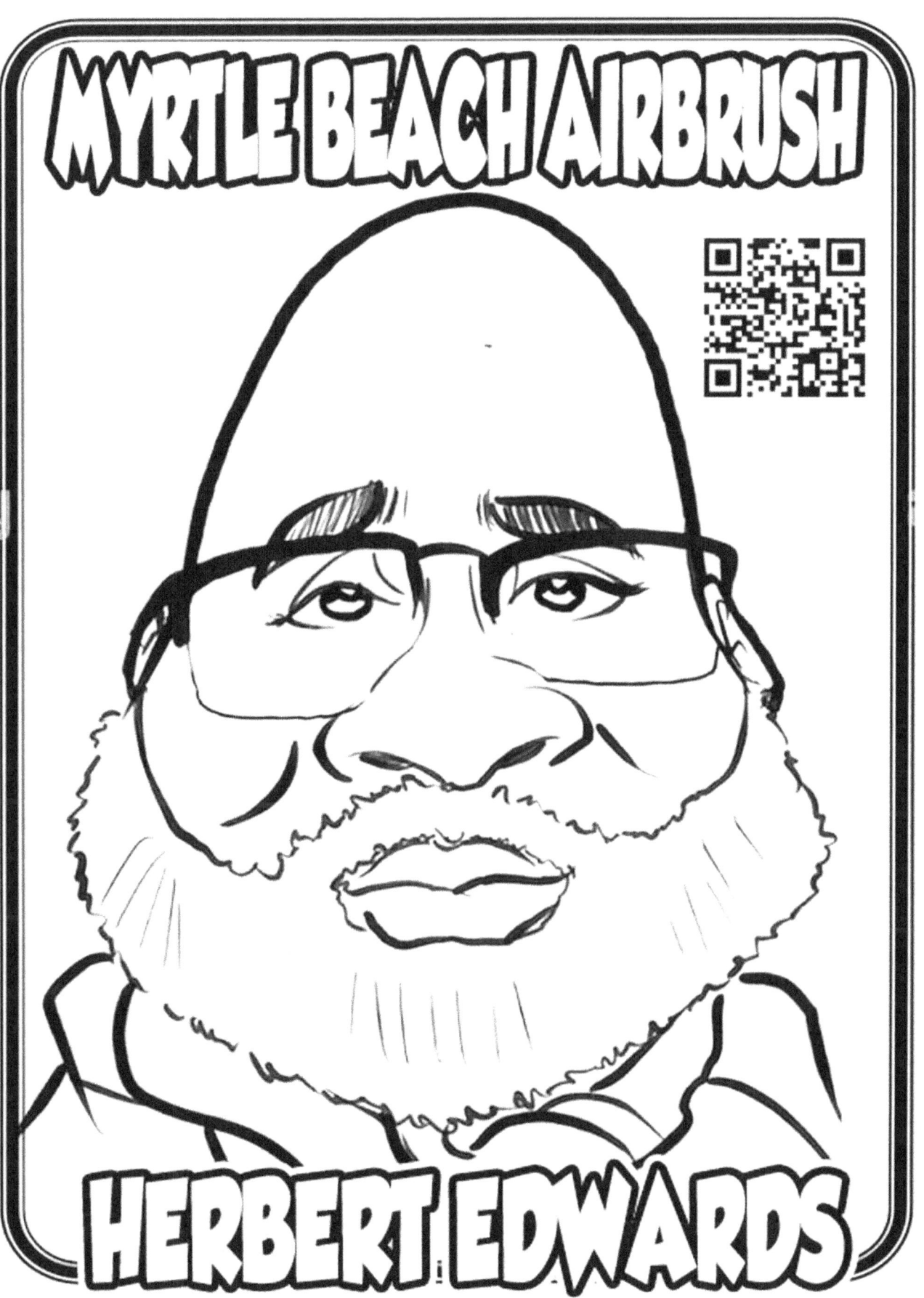

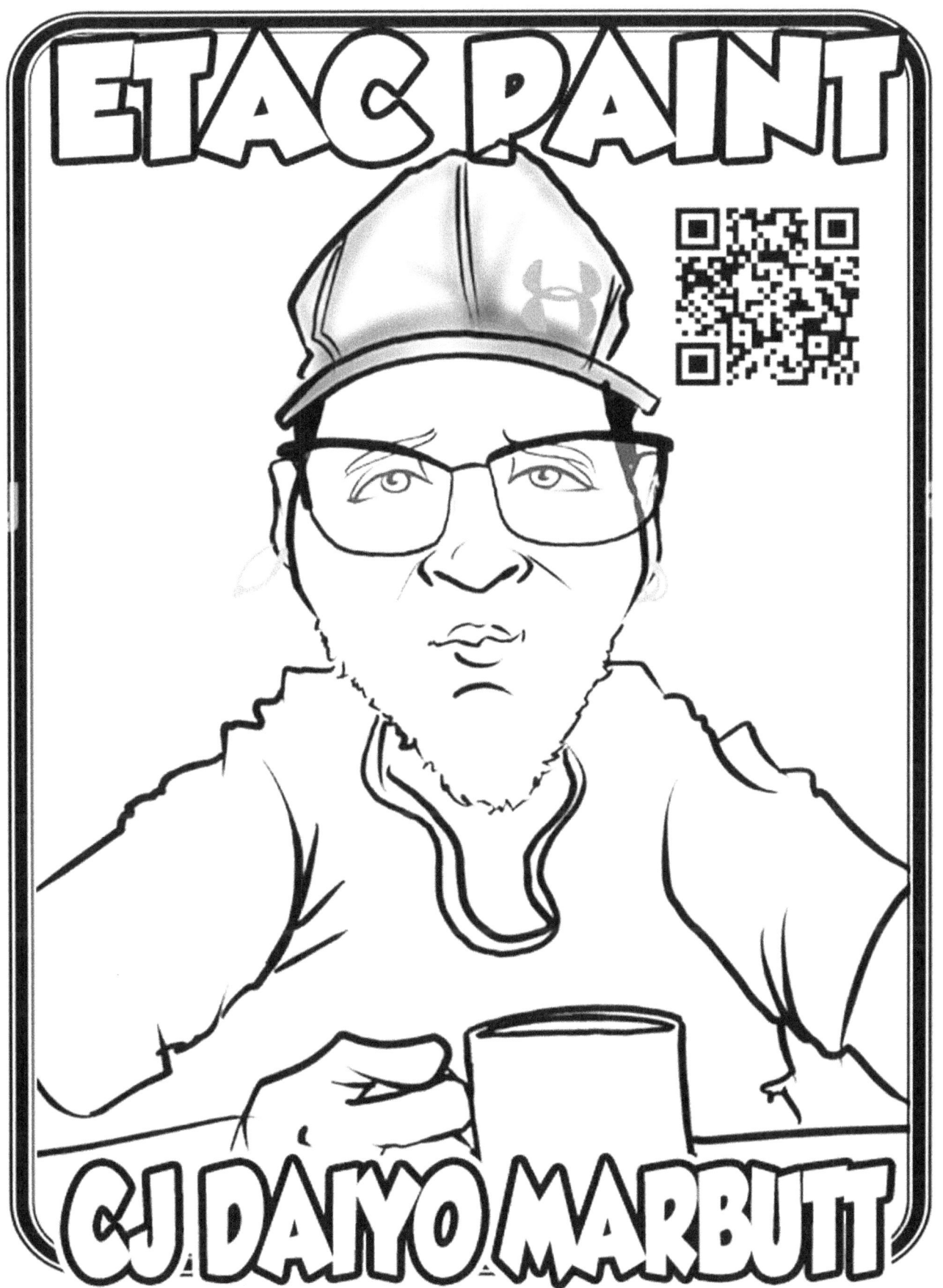

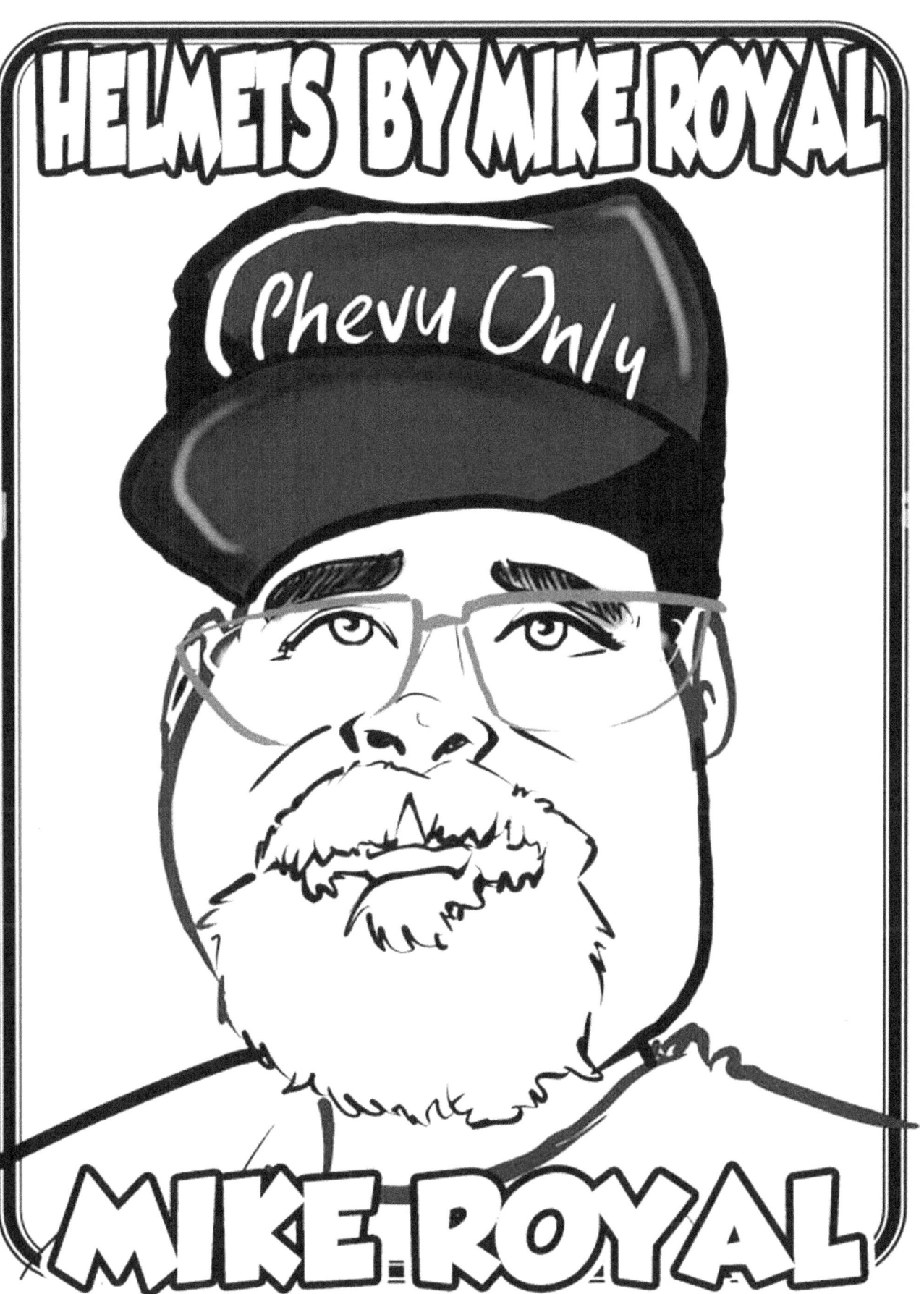

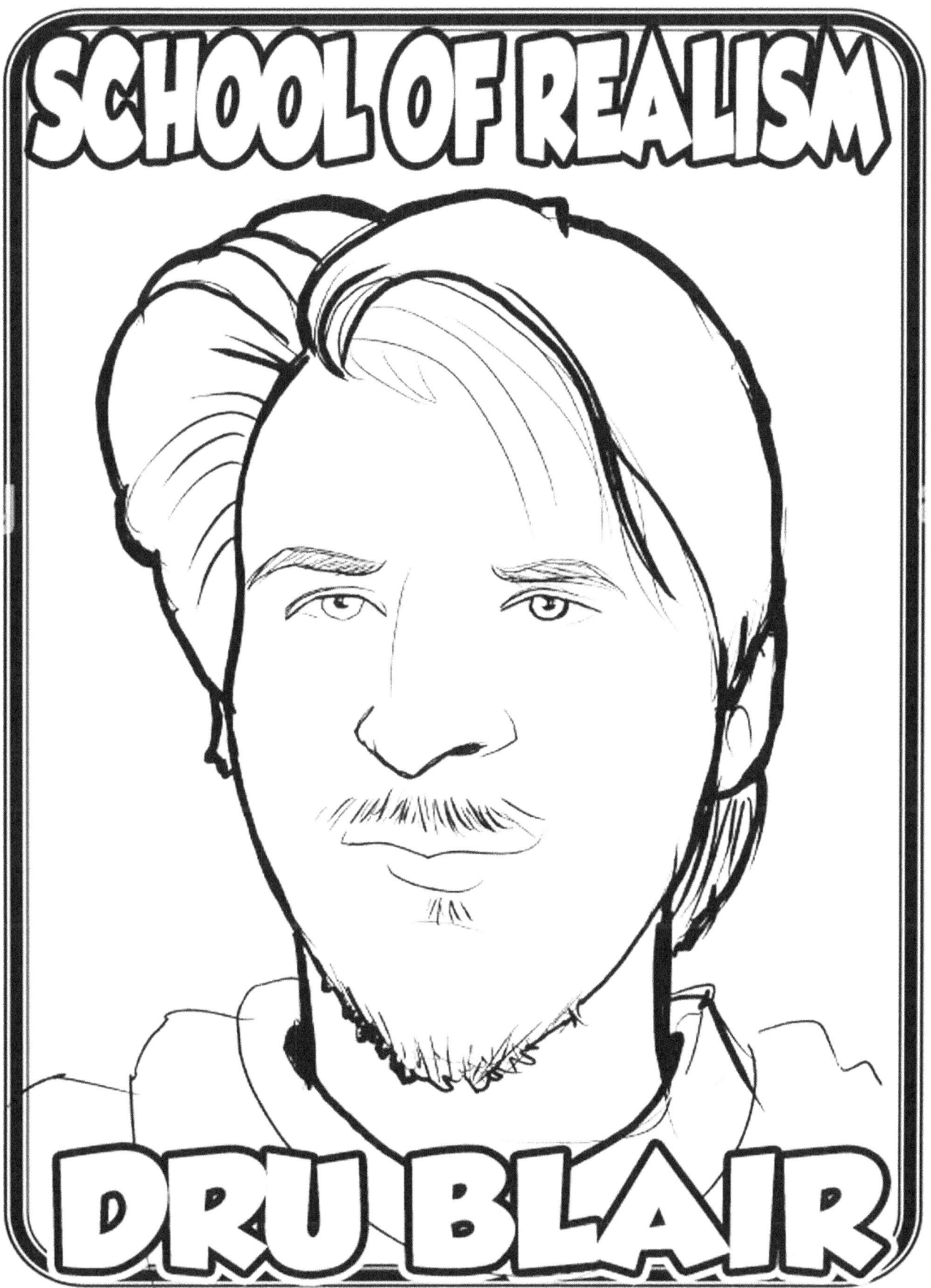

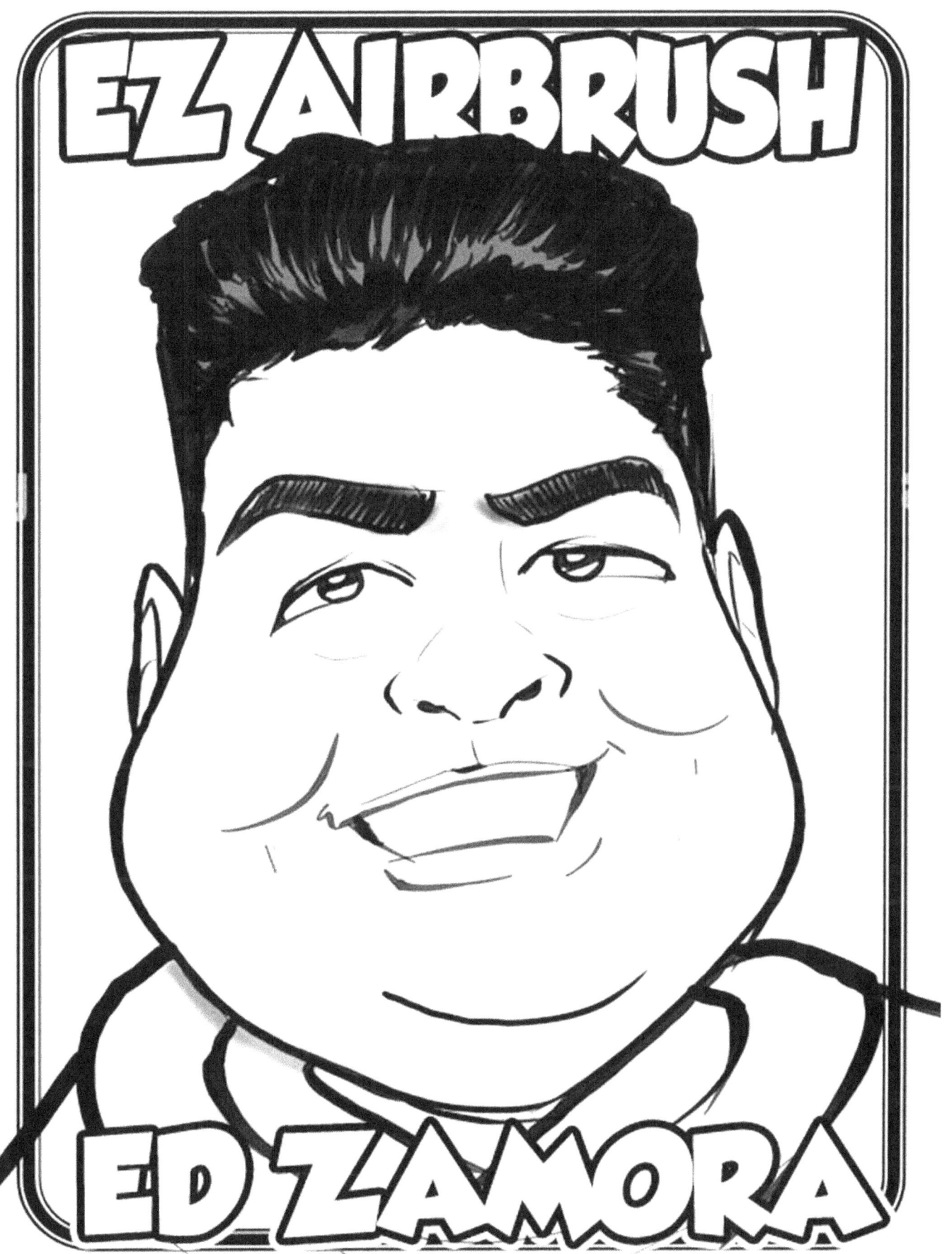

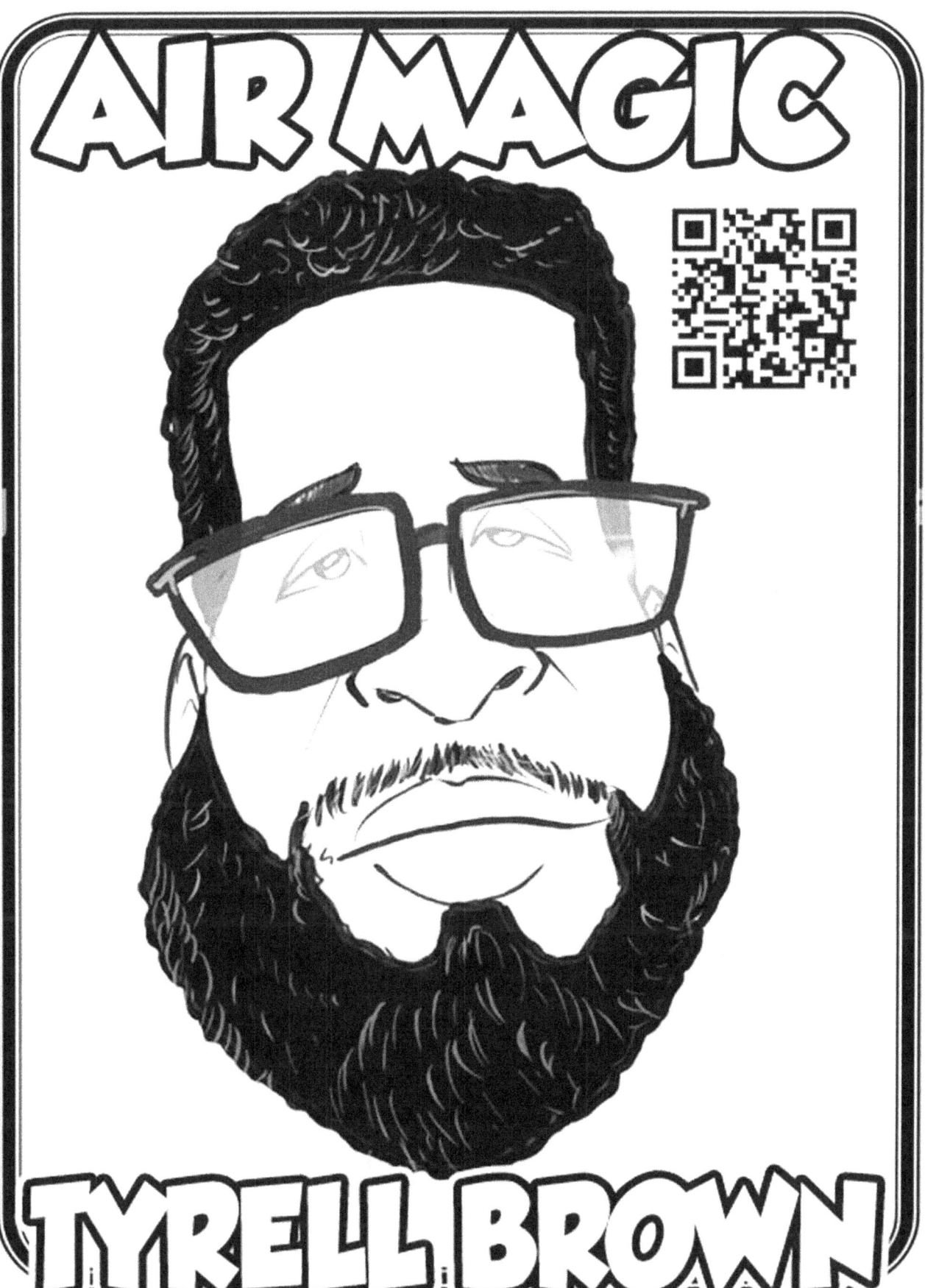

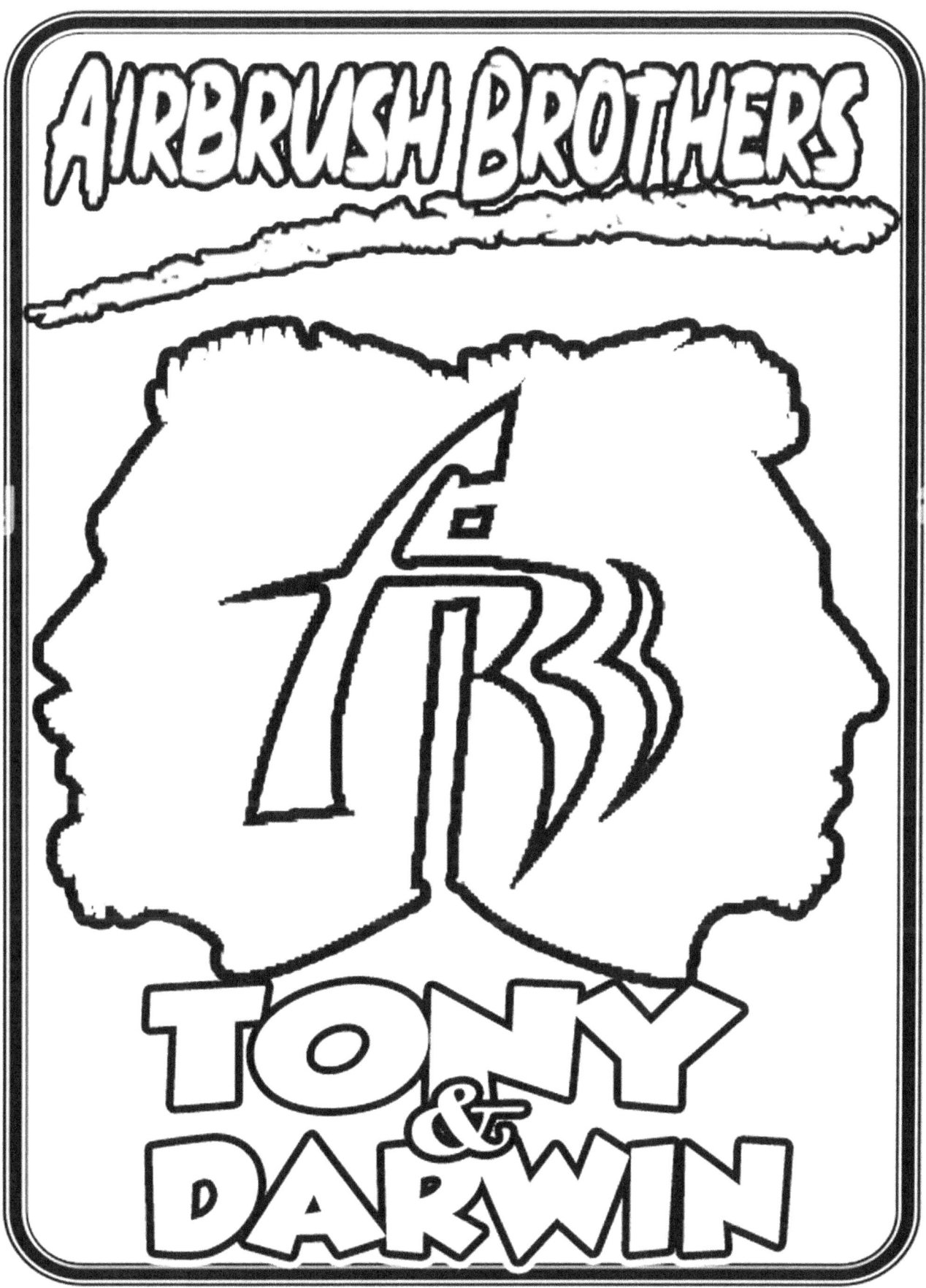

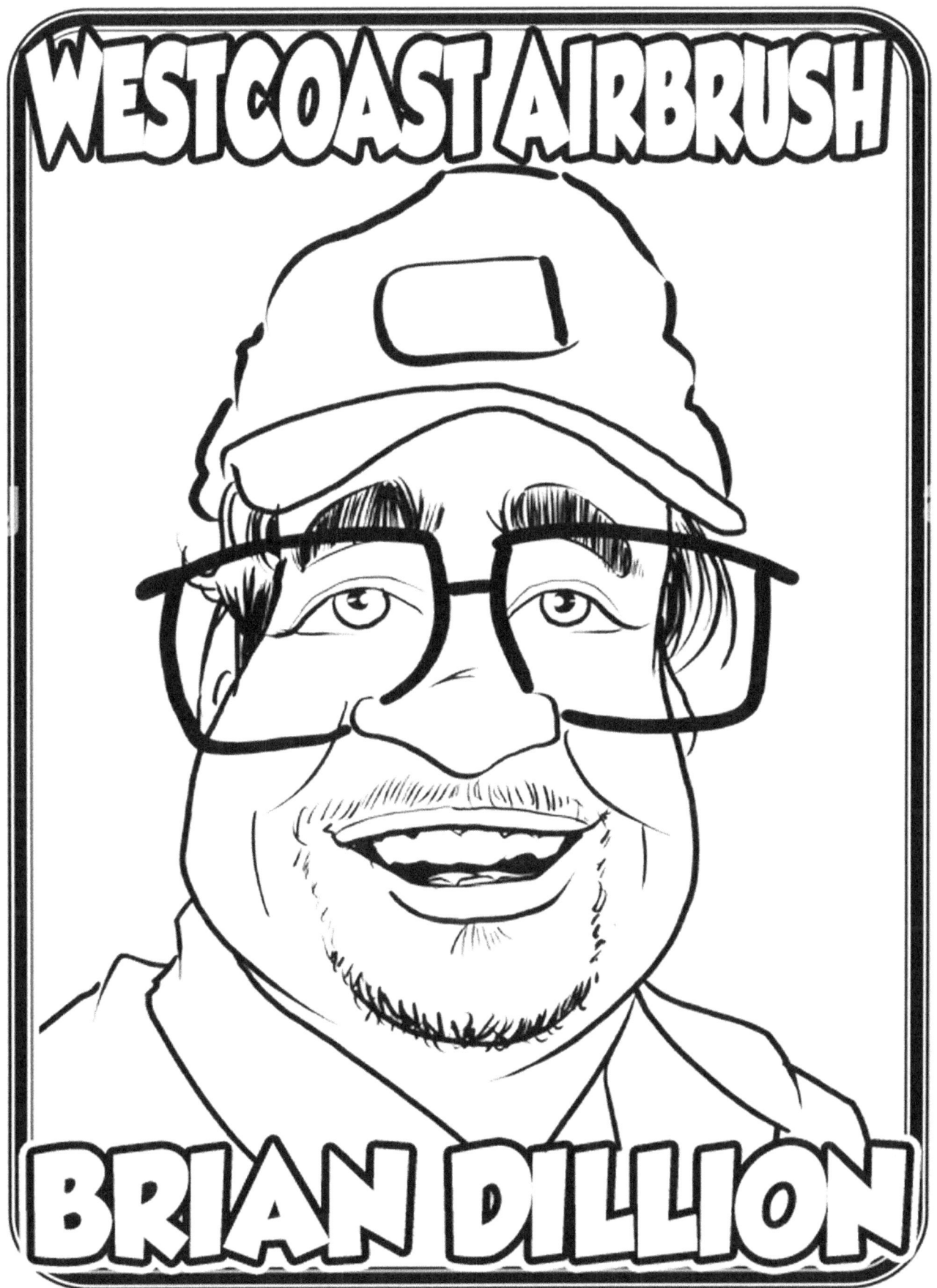

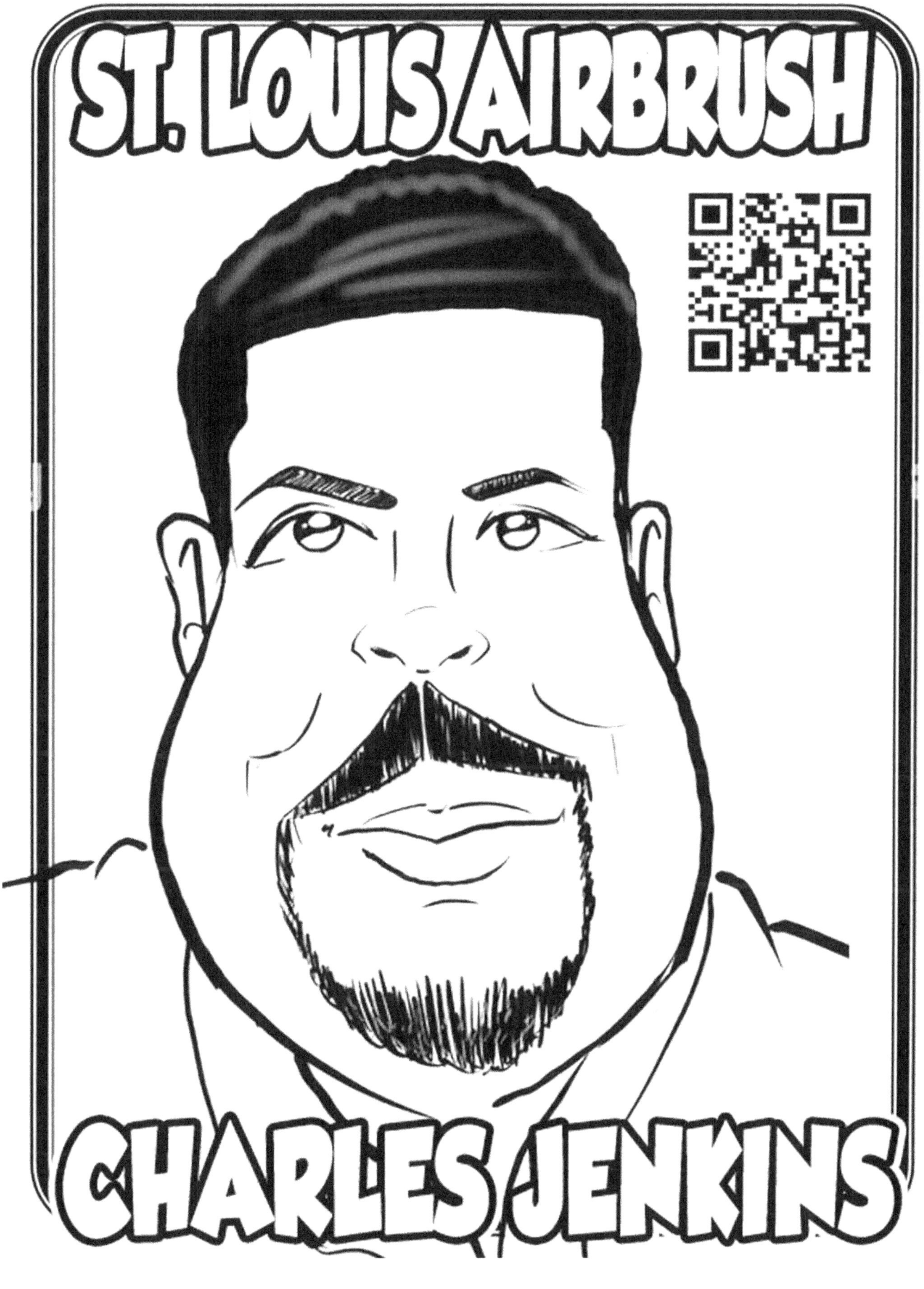
ST. LOUIS AIRBRUSH
CHARLES JENKINS

JSV ENTERTAINMENT

JOHN VARGAS

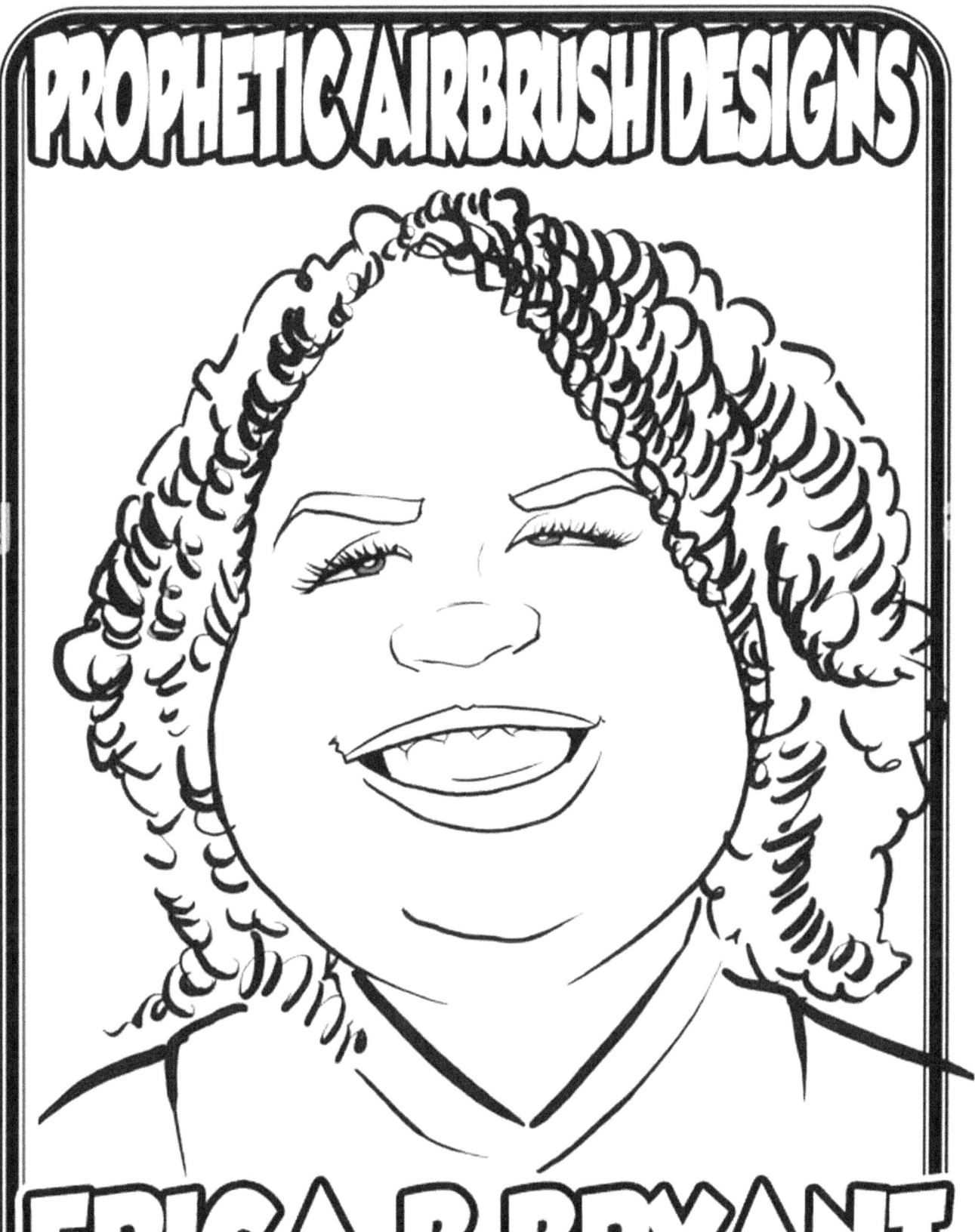

DALE THE AIBRUSH GUY

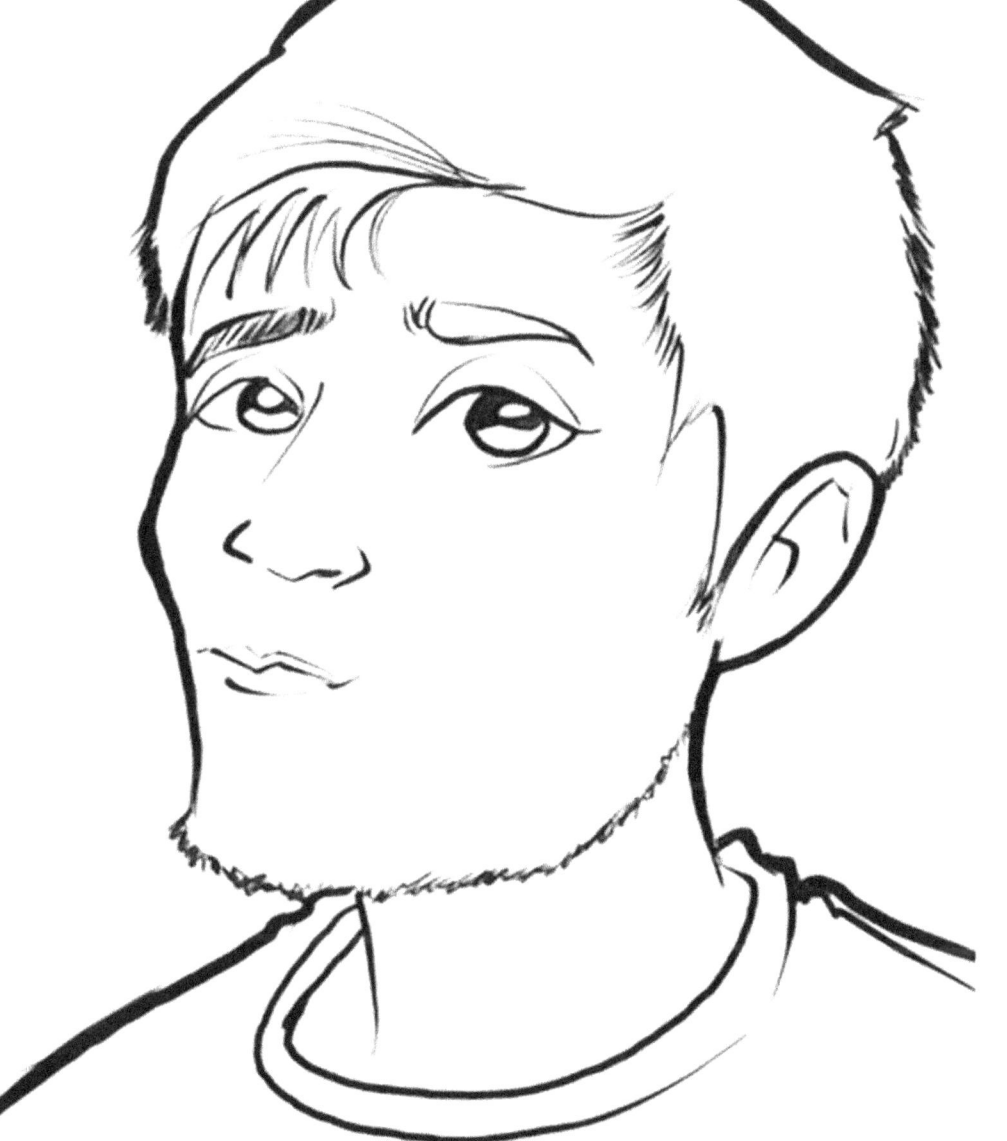

DALE JACKOWSKI

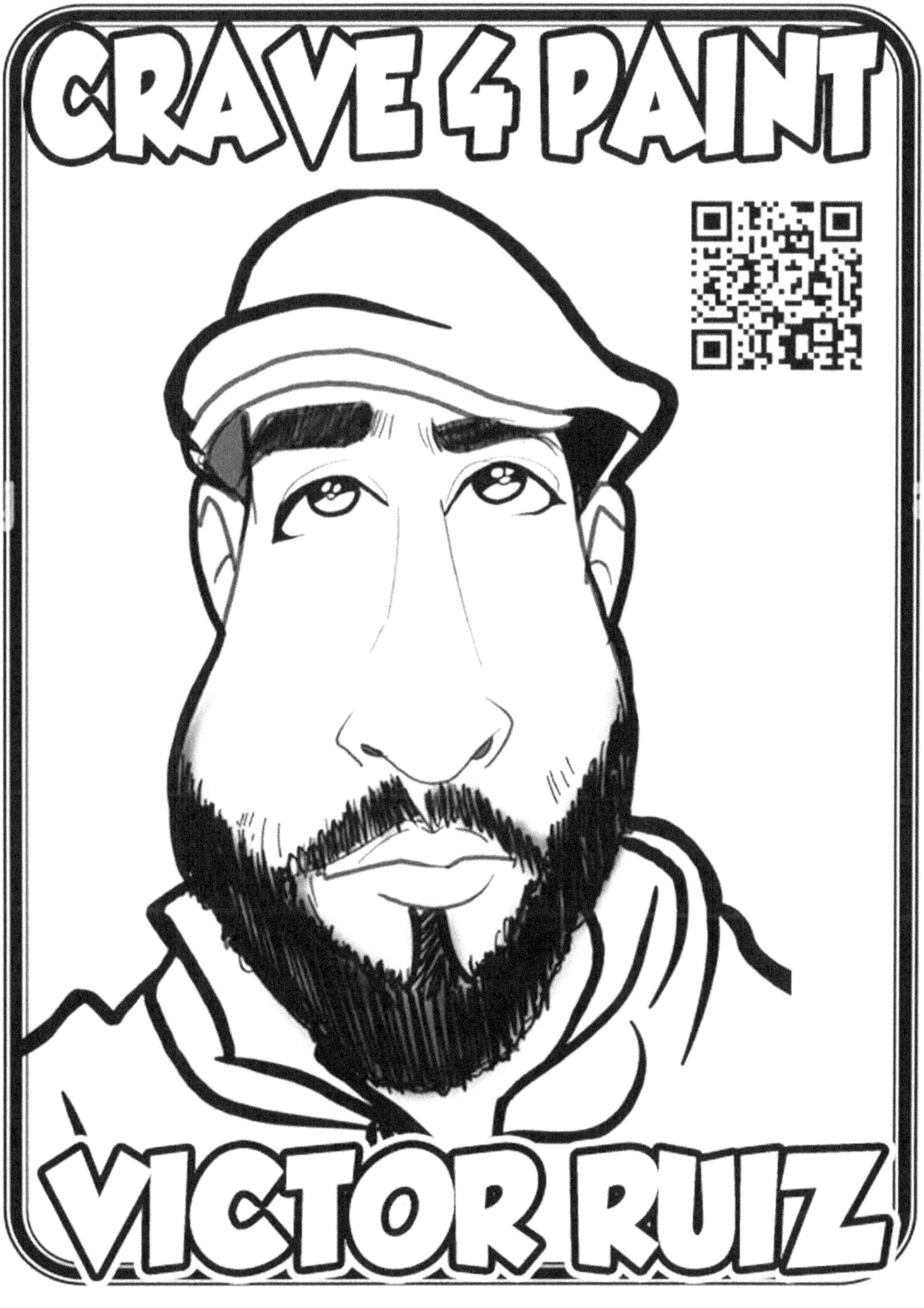
CRAVE 4 PAINT
VICTOR RUIZ

ARTISTIC MINDED AIRBRUSH

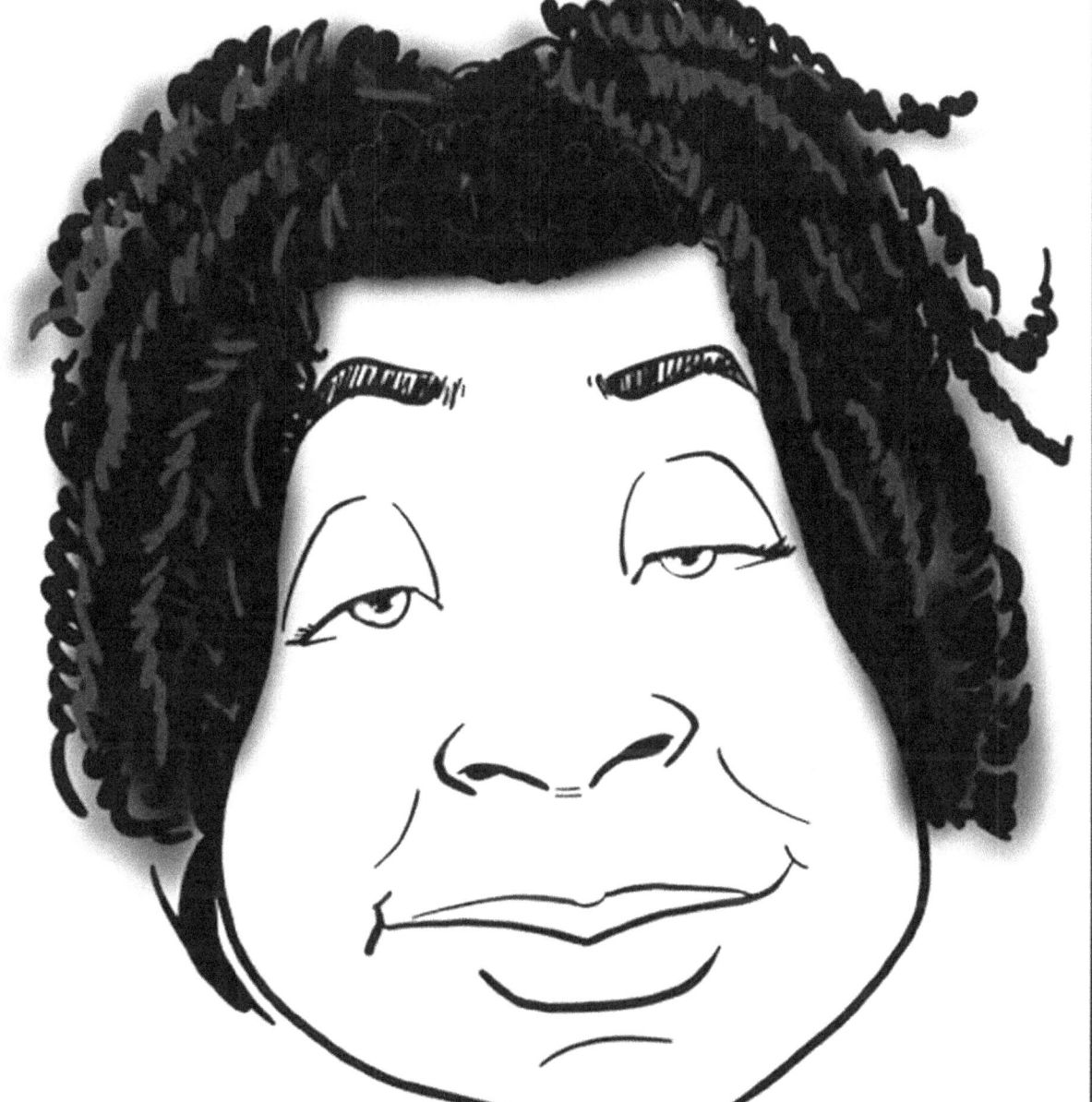

SANDTRA GOGGINS

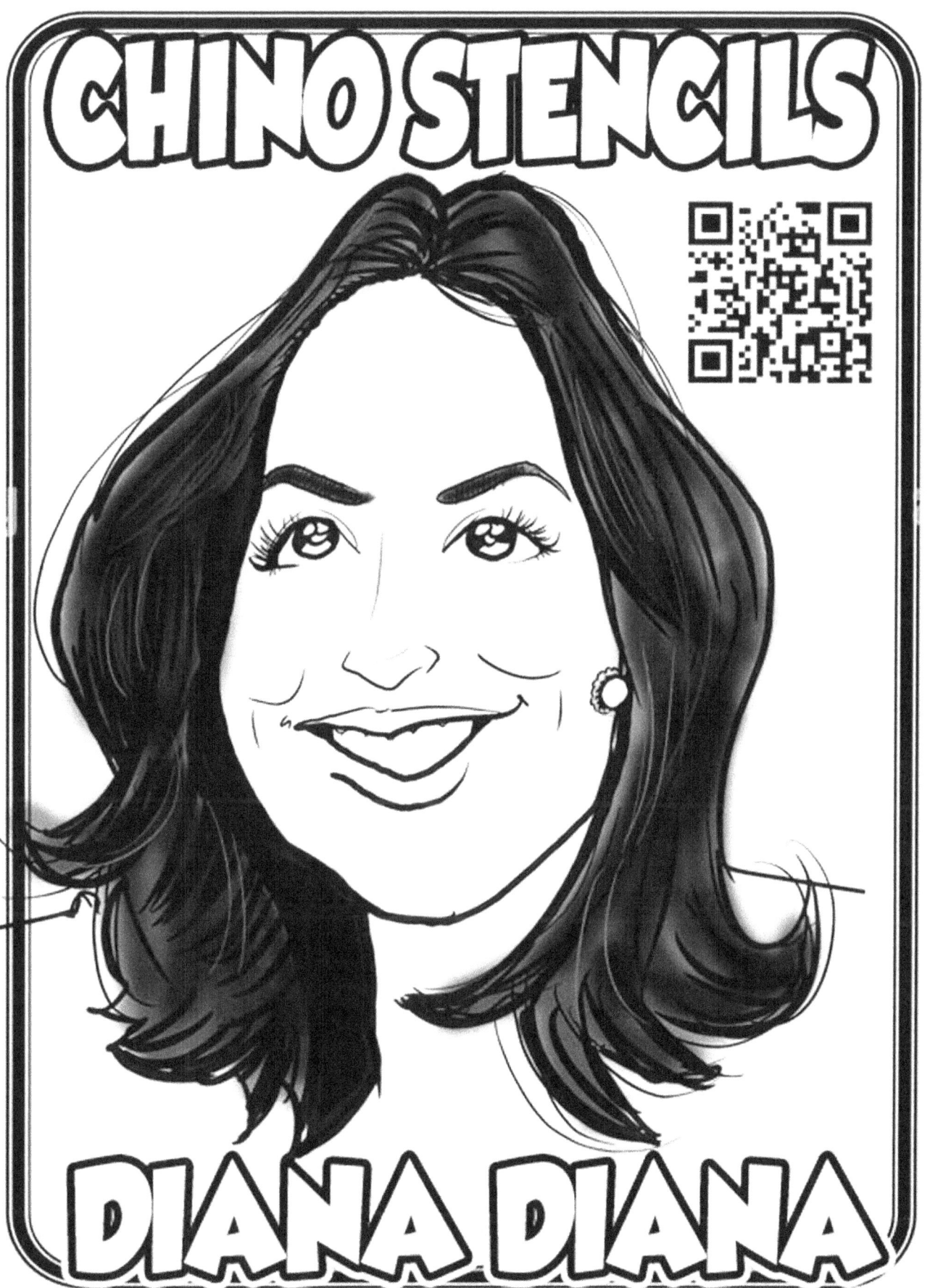

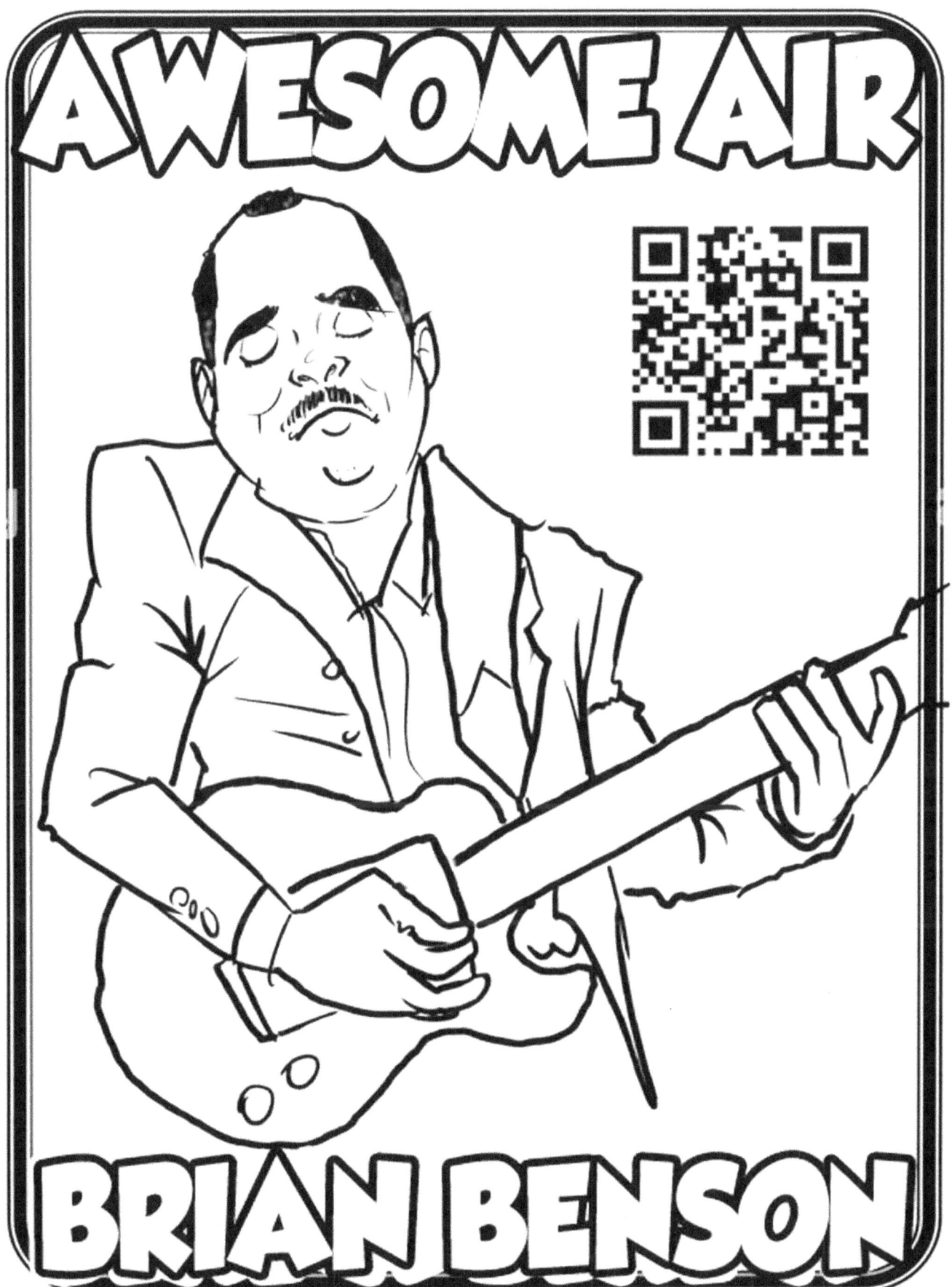

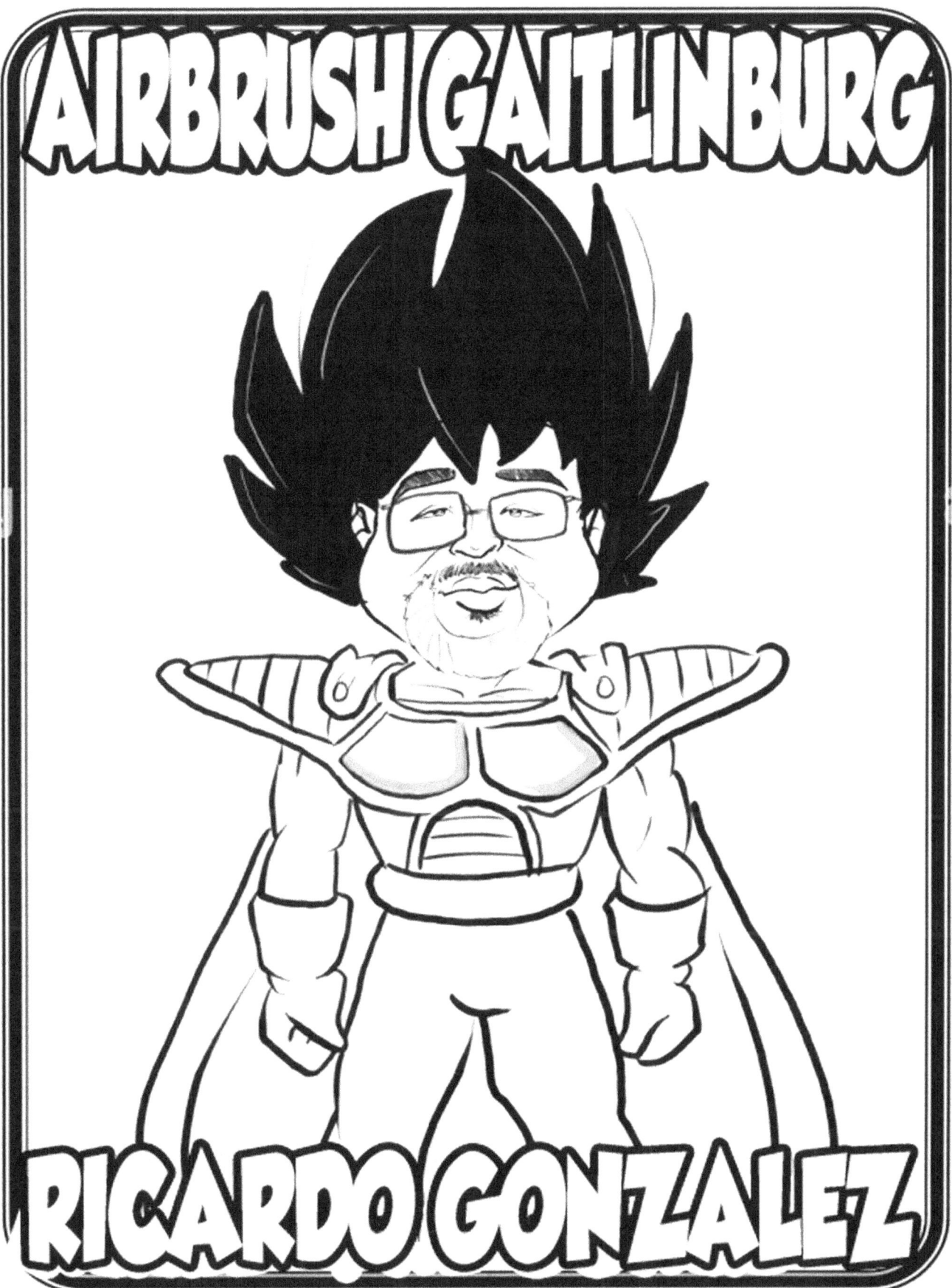

AIRBRUSH STUDIOS

PAUL LABELLE

AIRBRUSH STUDIOS

ARRIN VANGUARD

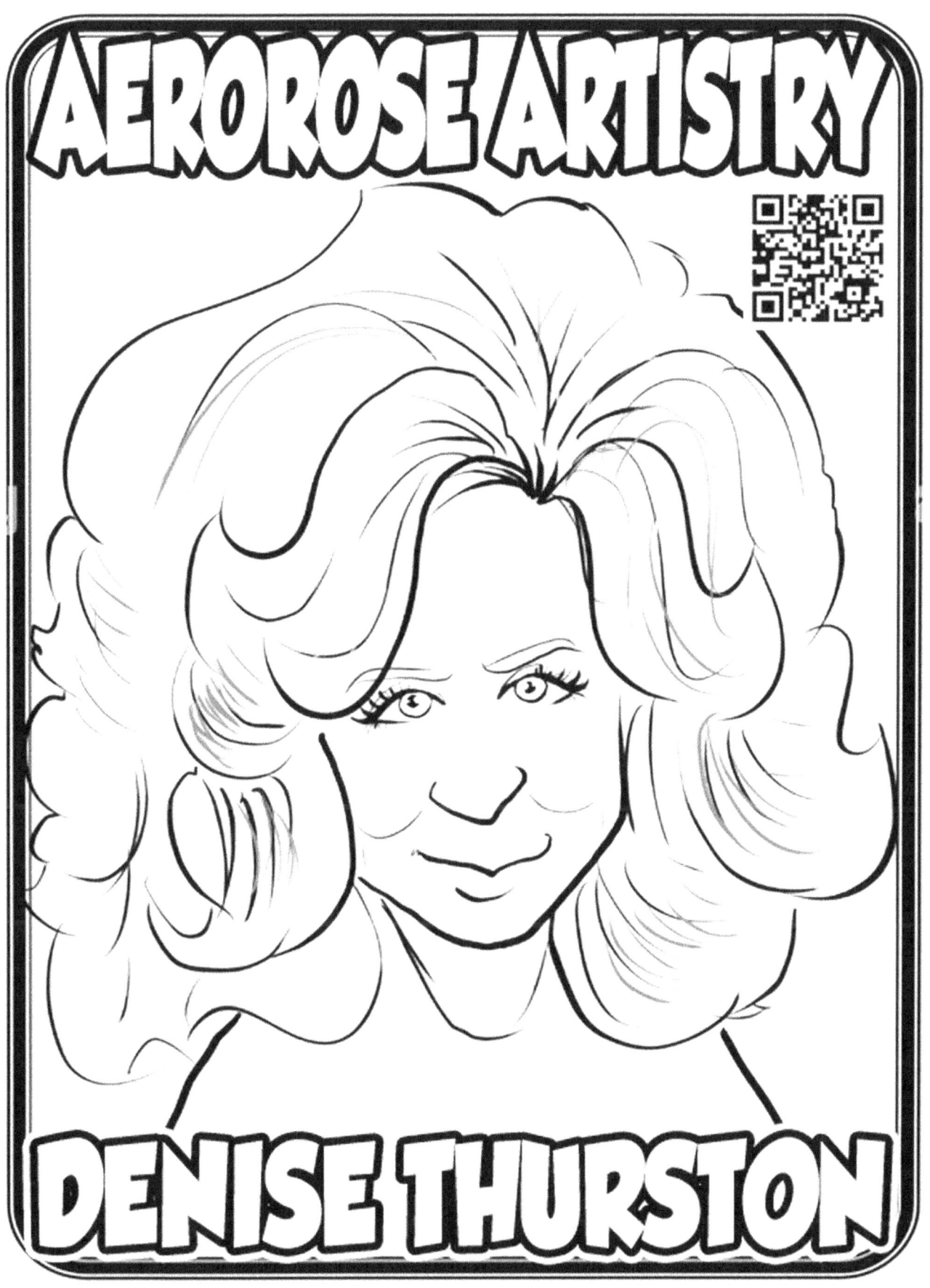

SILLY FARMS

HEATHER GREEN

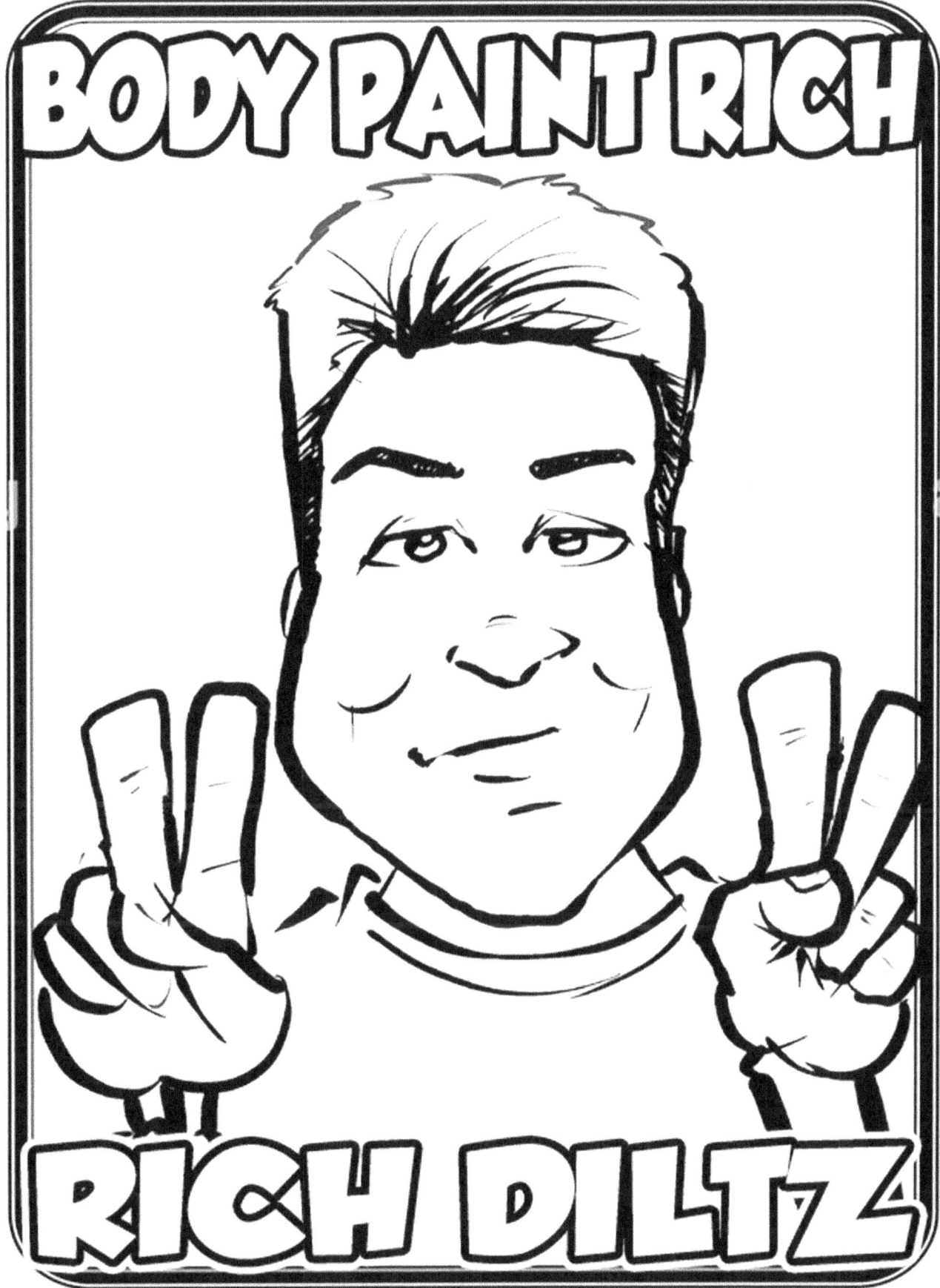

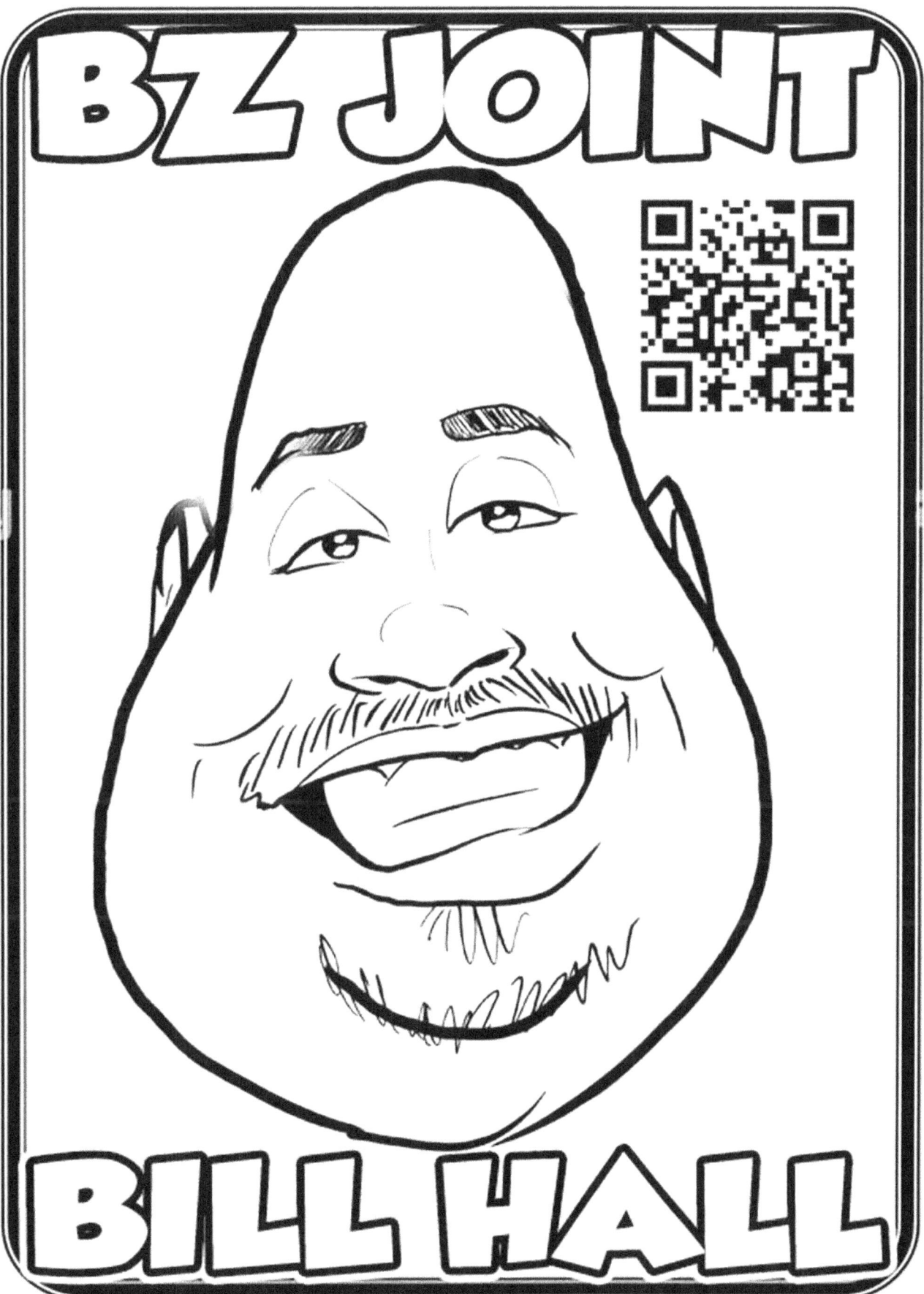

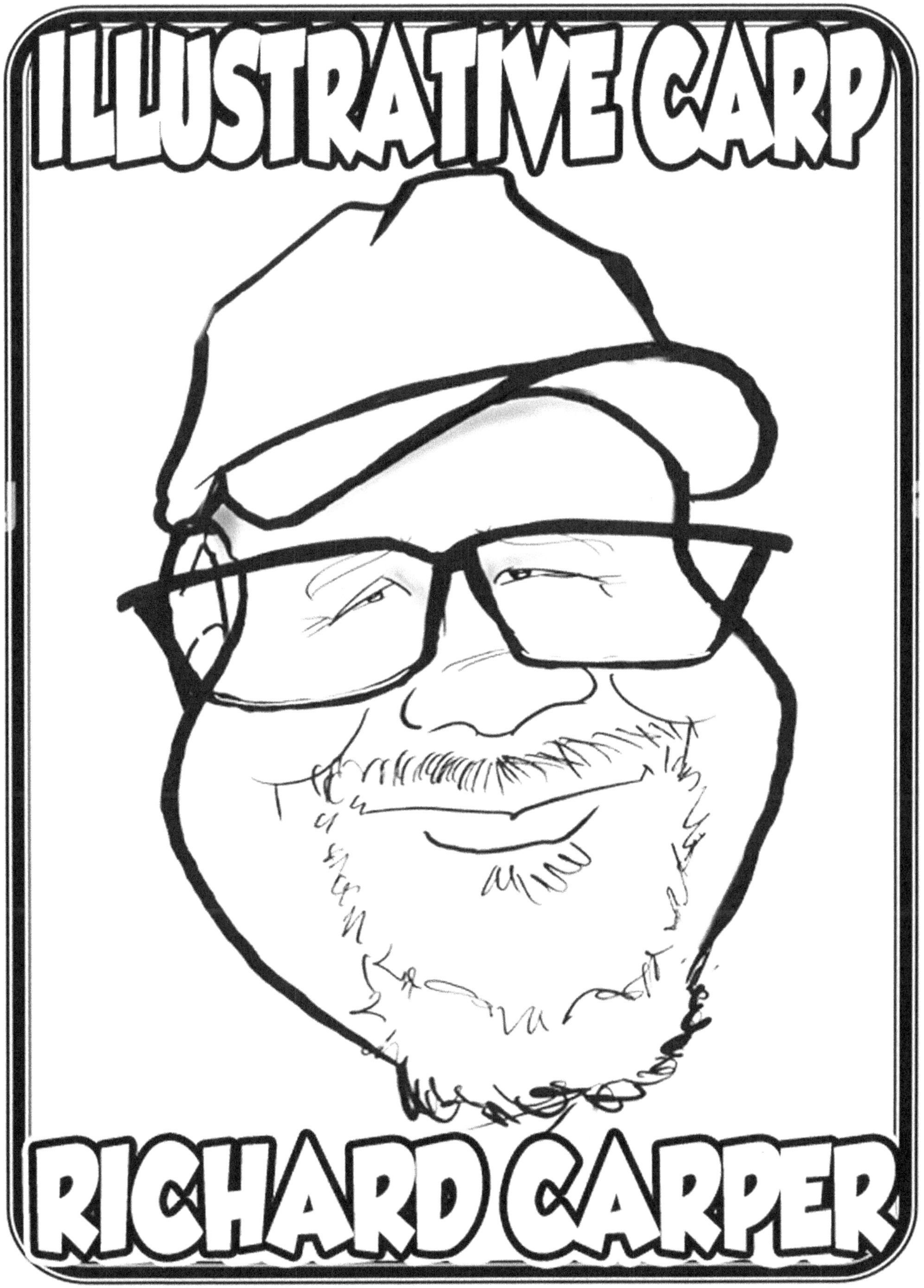
ILLUSTRATIVE CARP
RICHARD CARPER

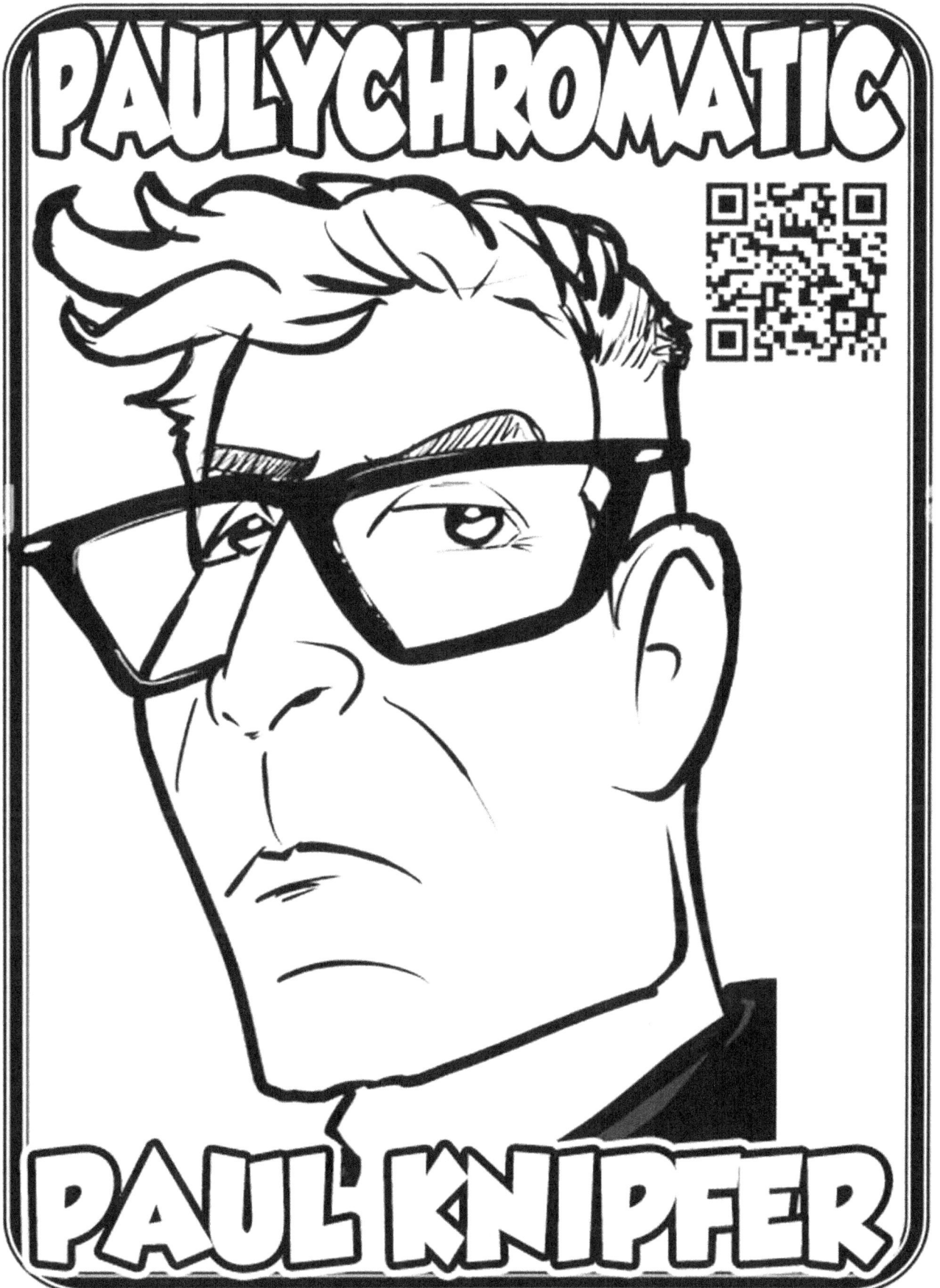

CENLA CUSTOMS

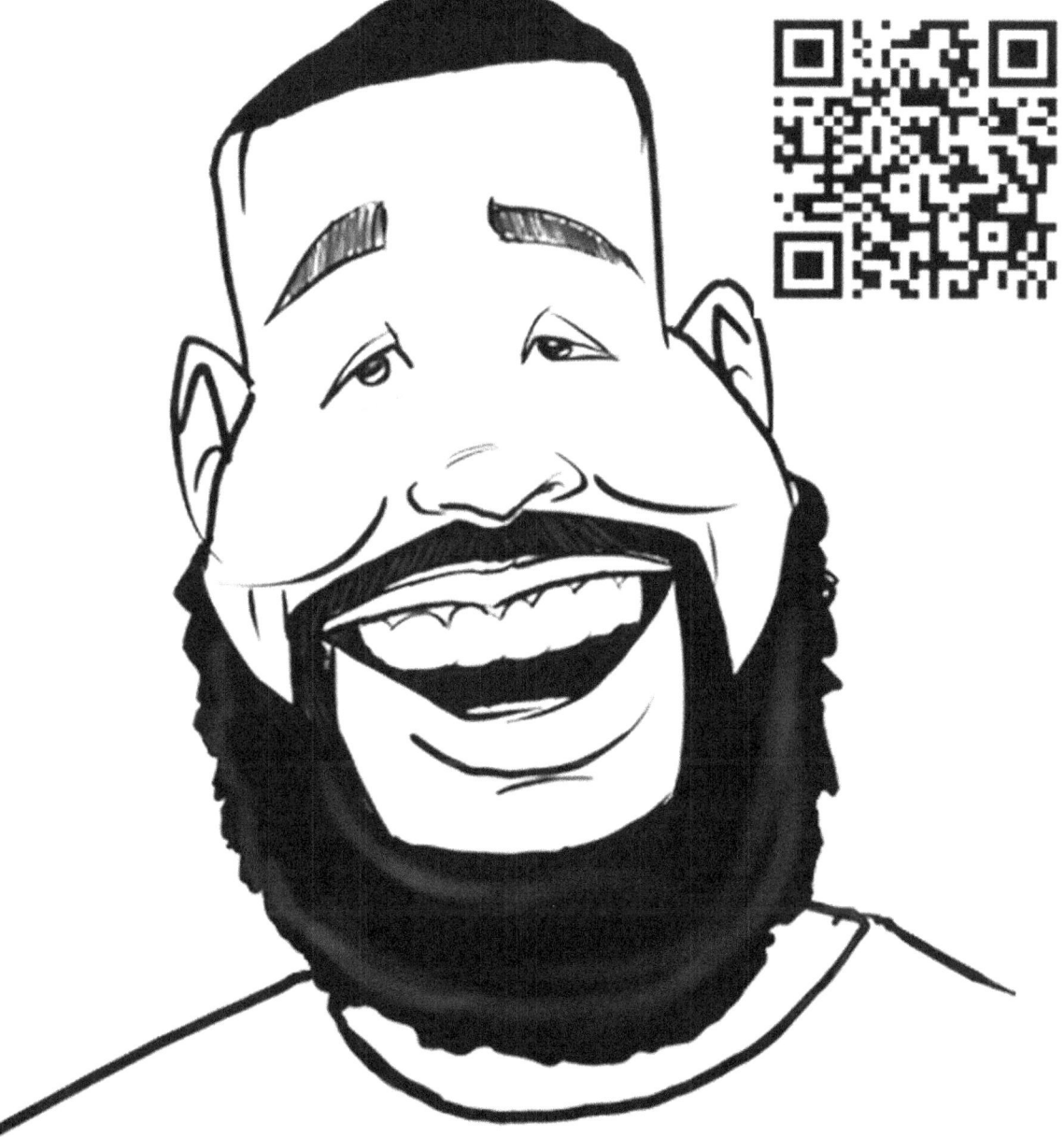

TERRANCE PHILLIPS SR.

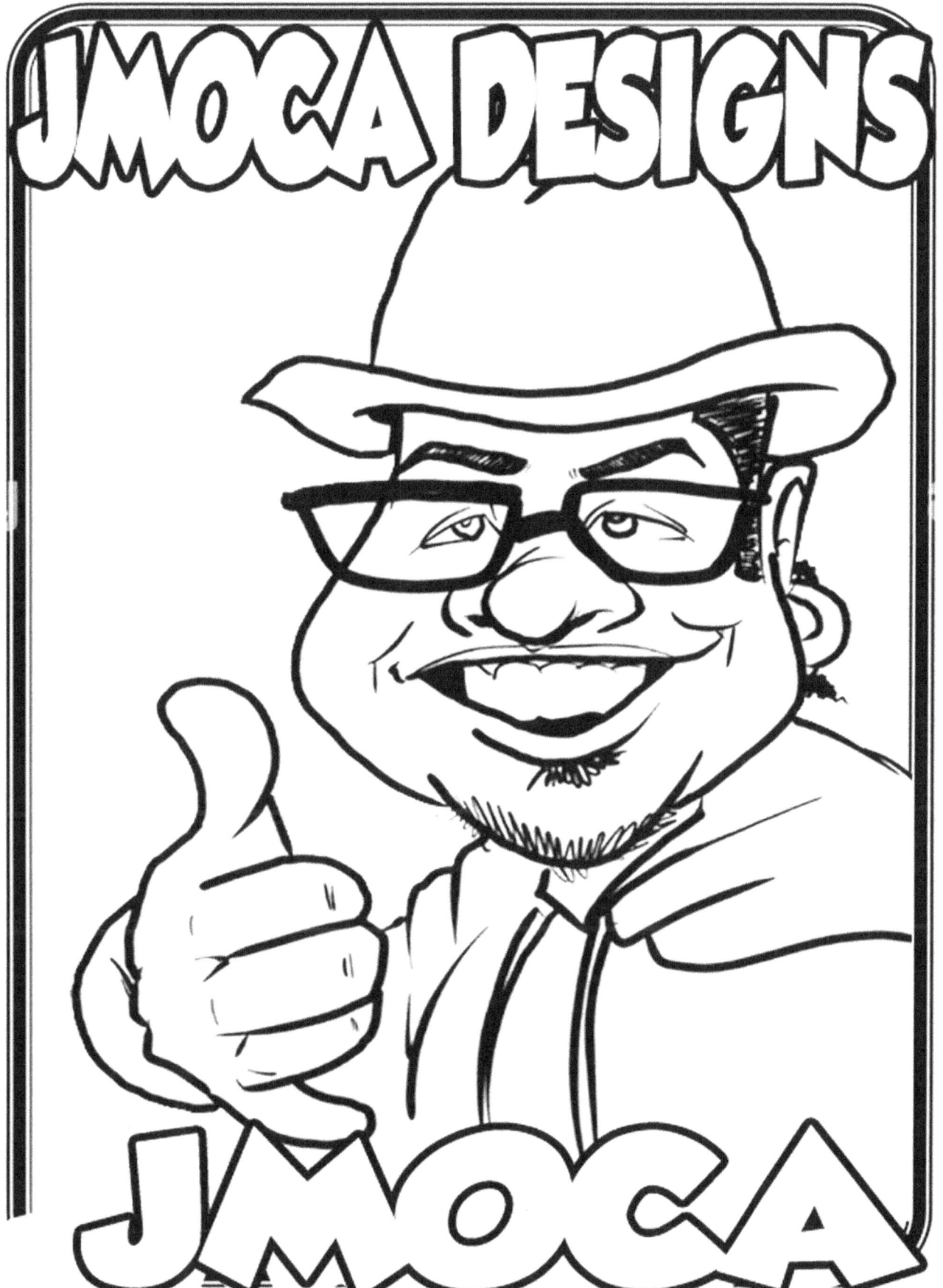

ANOINTED AIR

RUBEN FIGUEROA

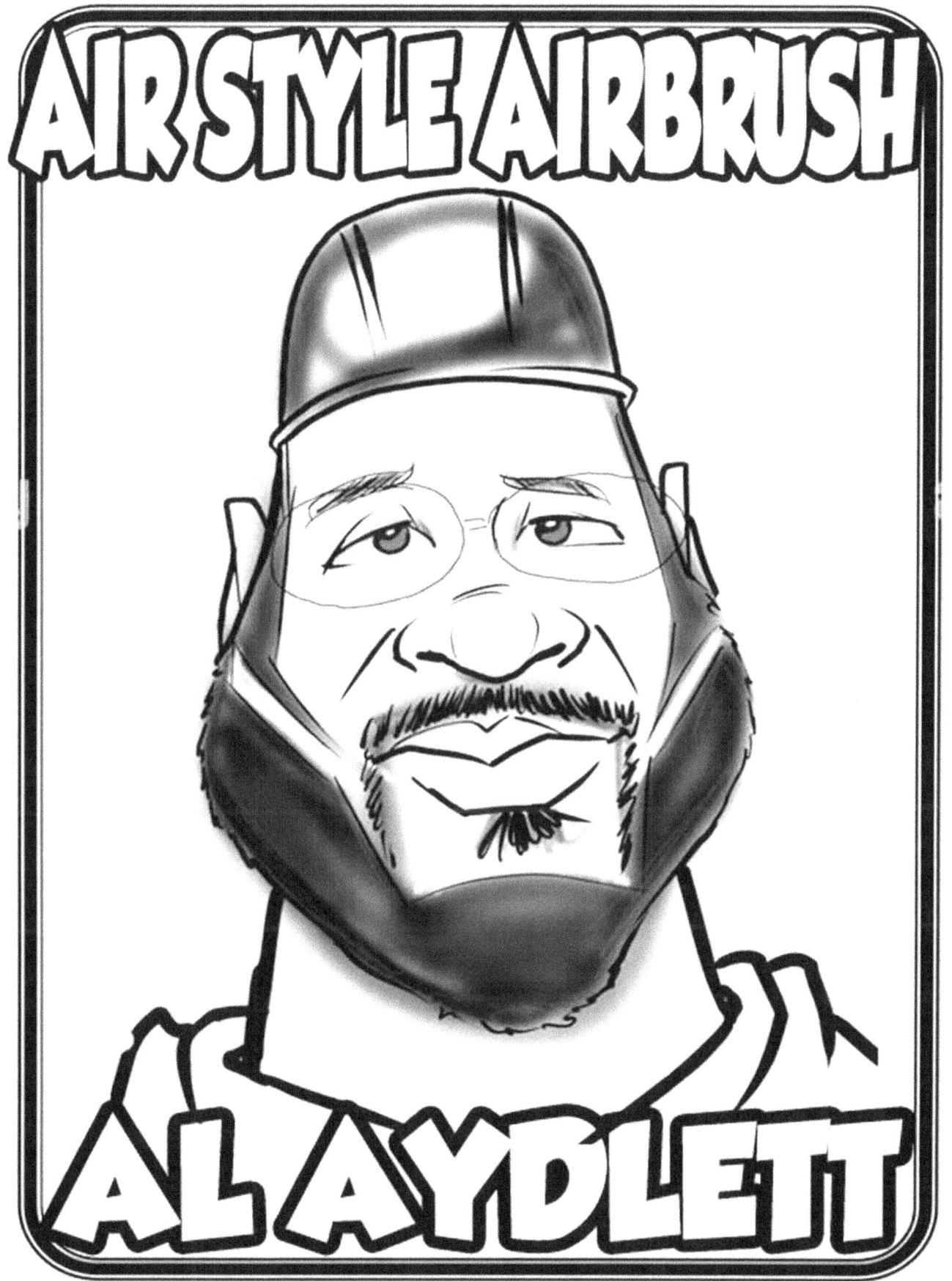

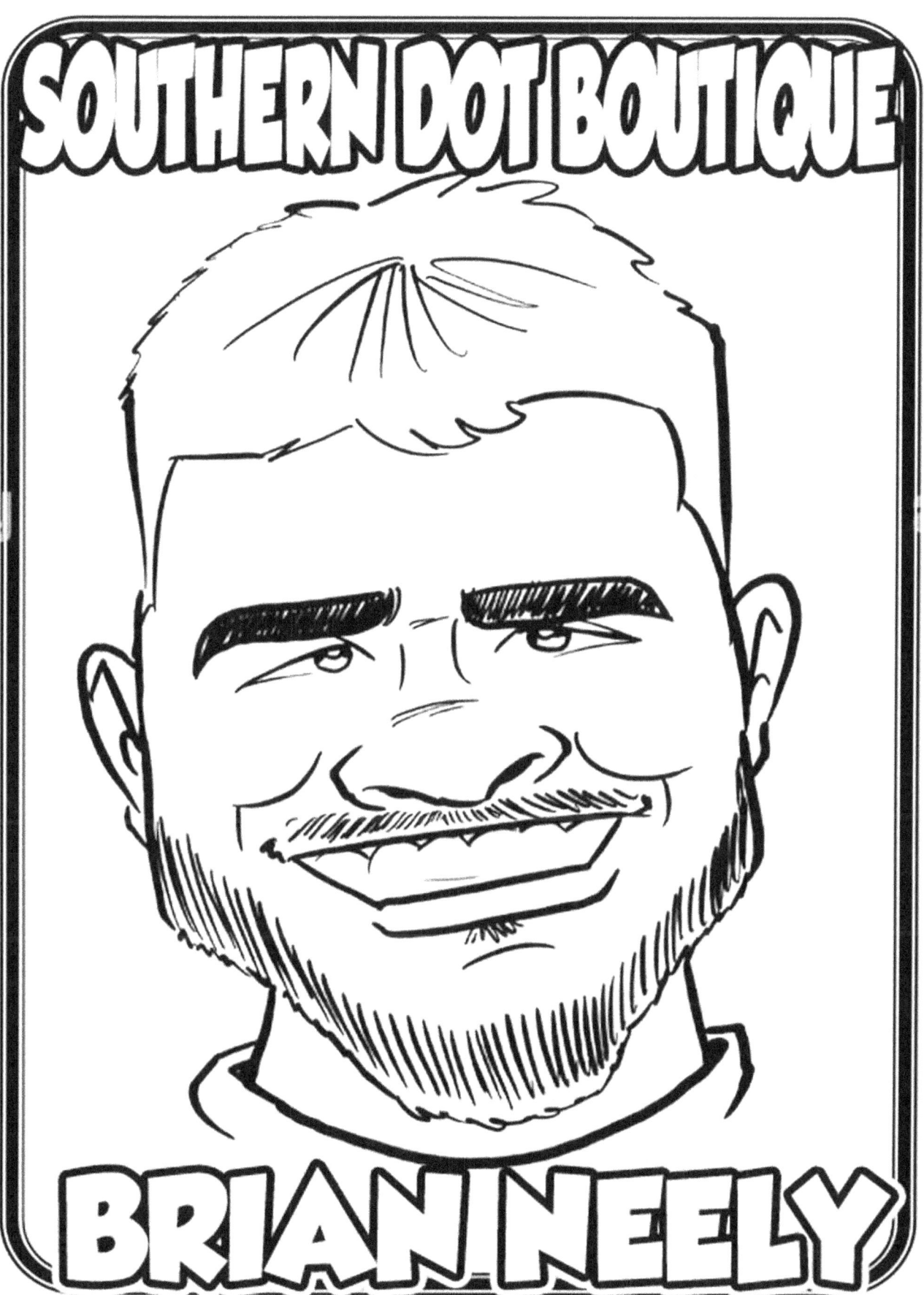

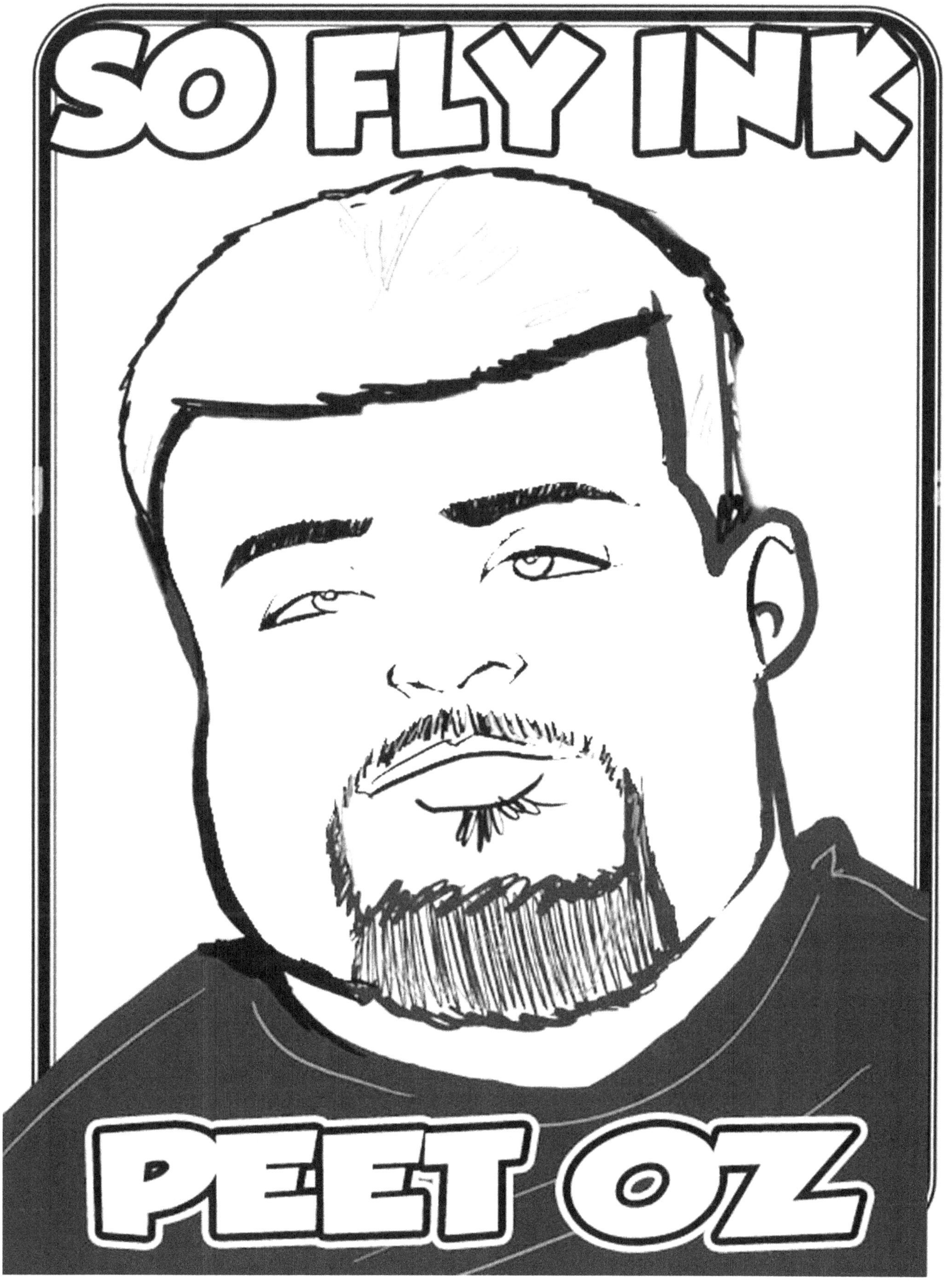
SO FLY INK
PEET OZ

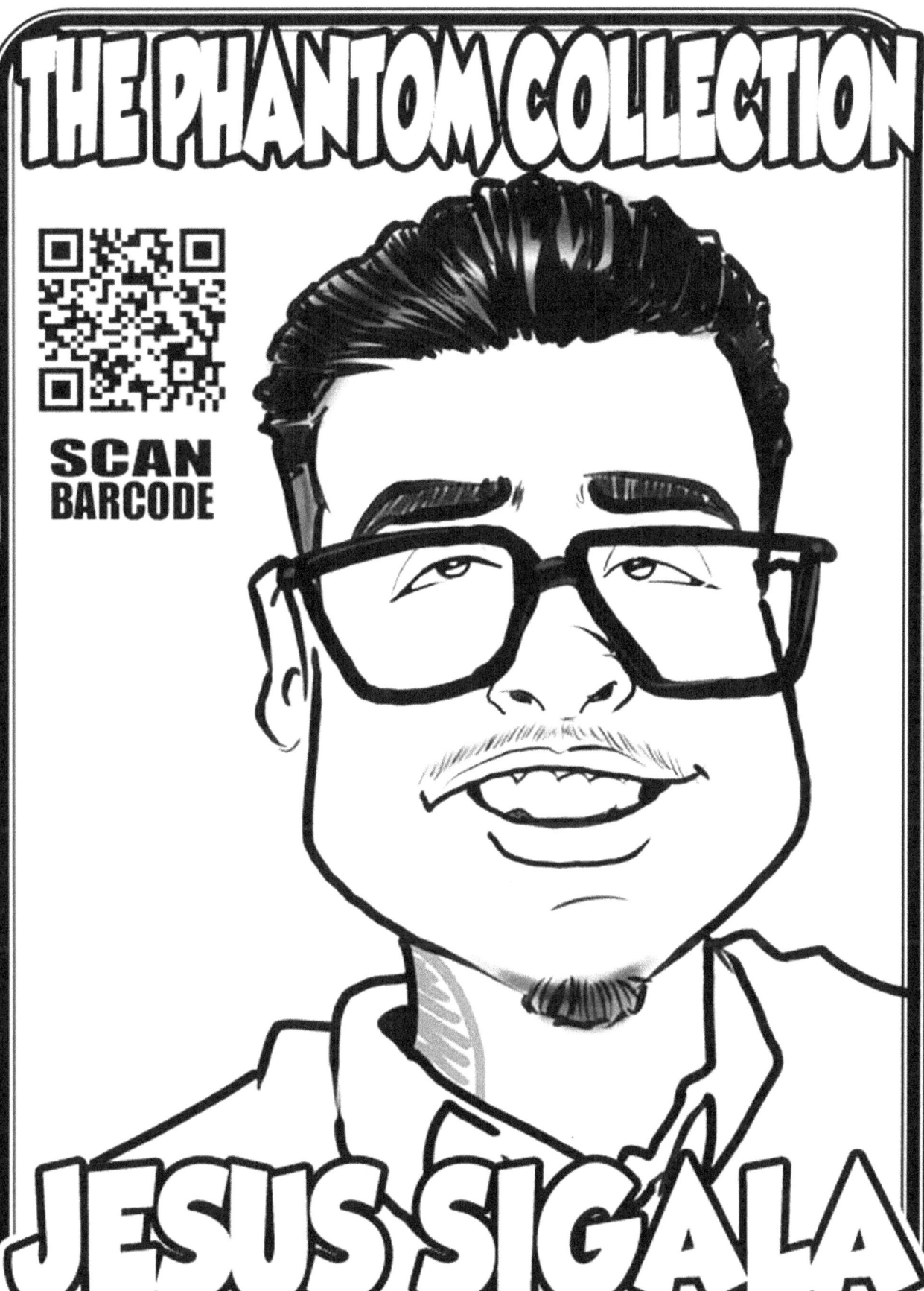

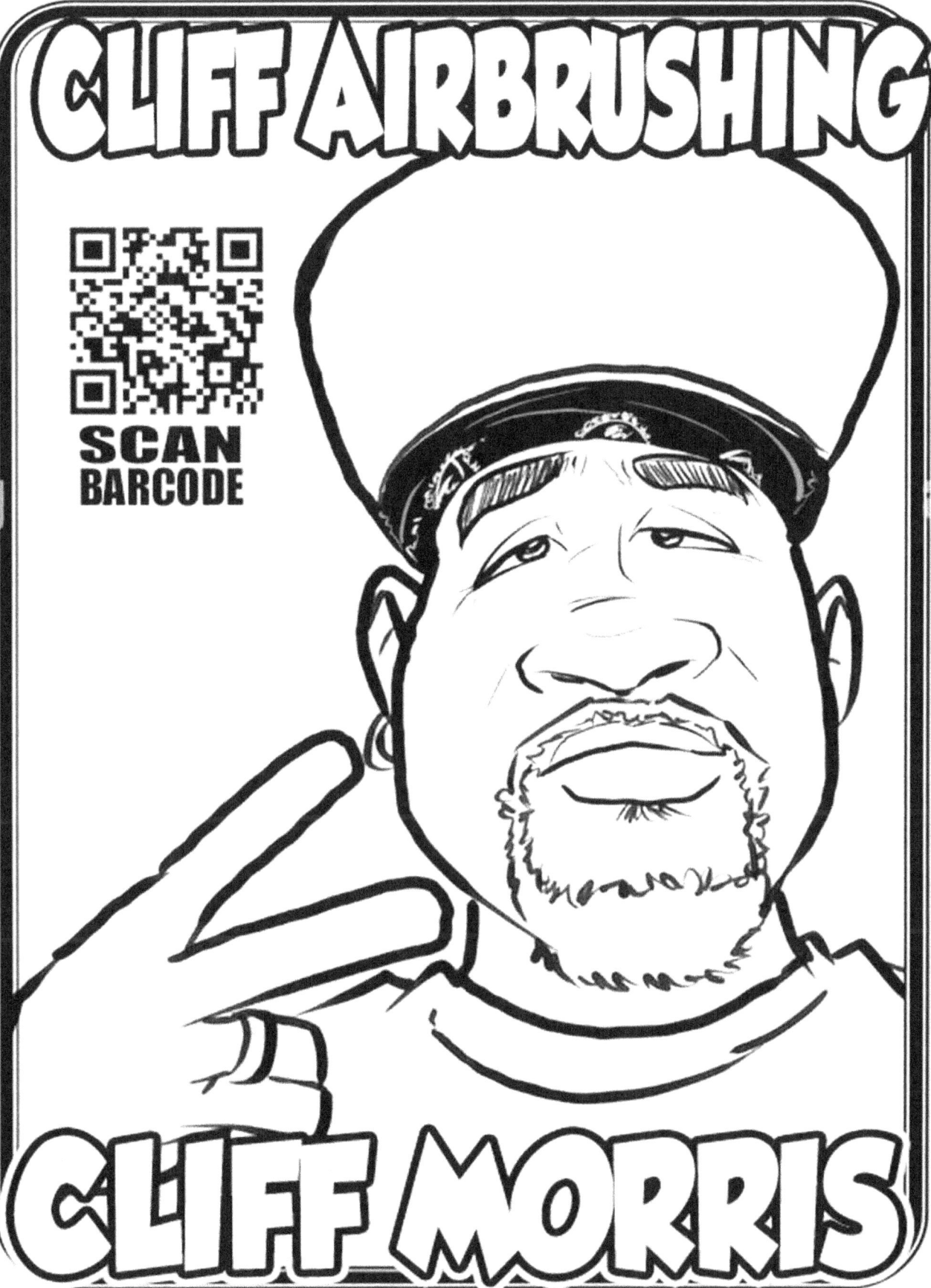

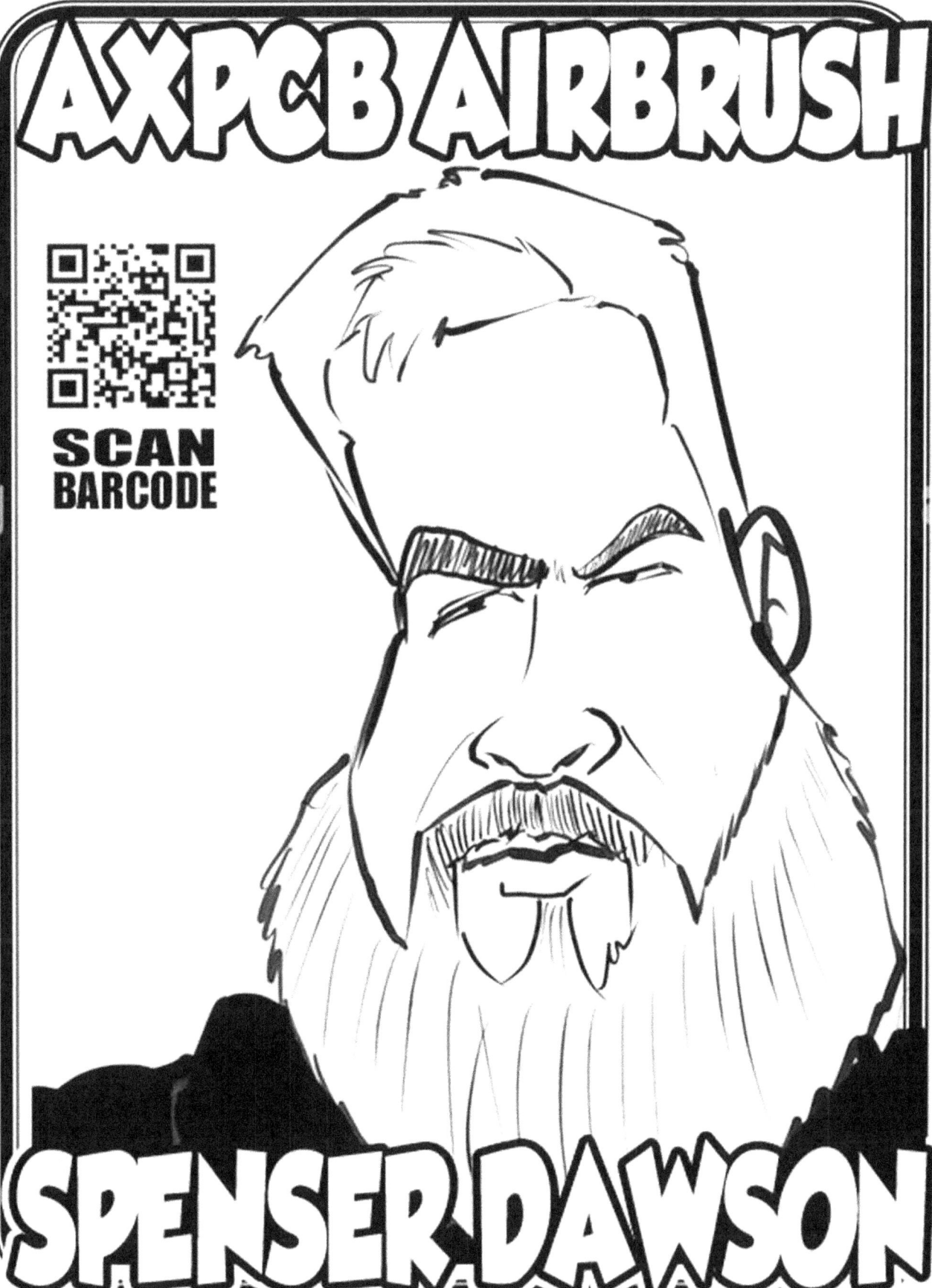

PASTRANA UNLIMITED LLC

SCAN
BARCODE
FOR VIDEO

ALAN PASTRANA

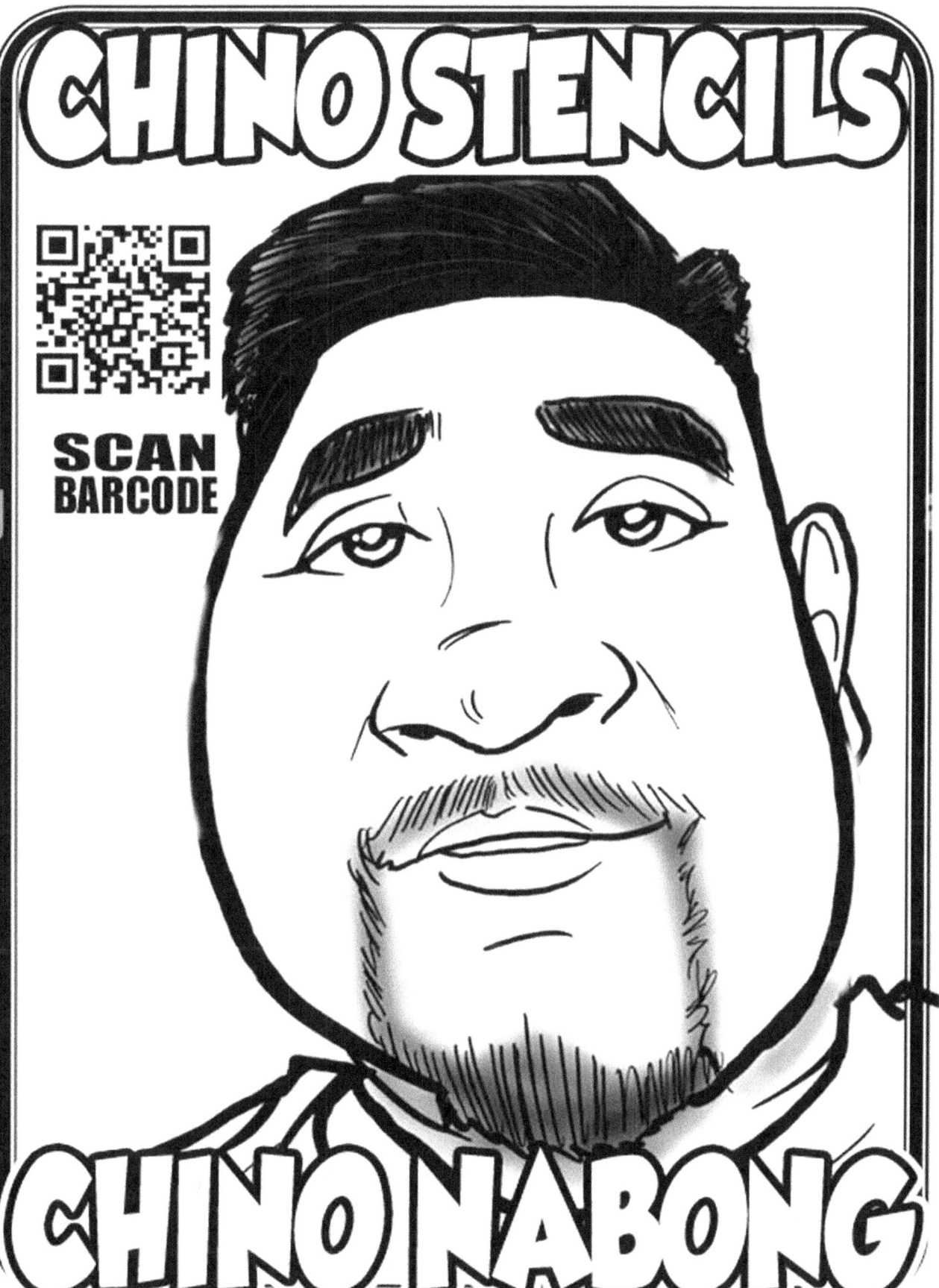

CHINO STENCILS

SCAN BARCODE

CHINO NABONG

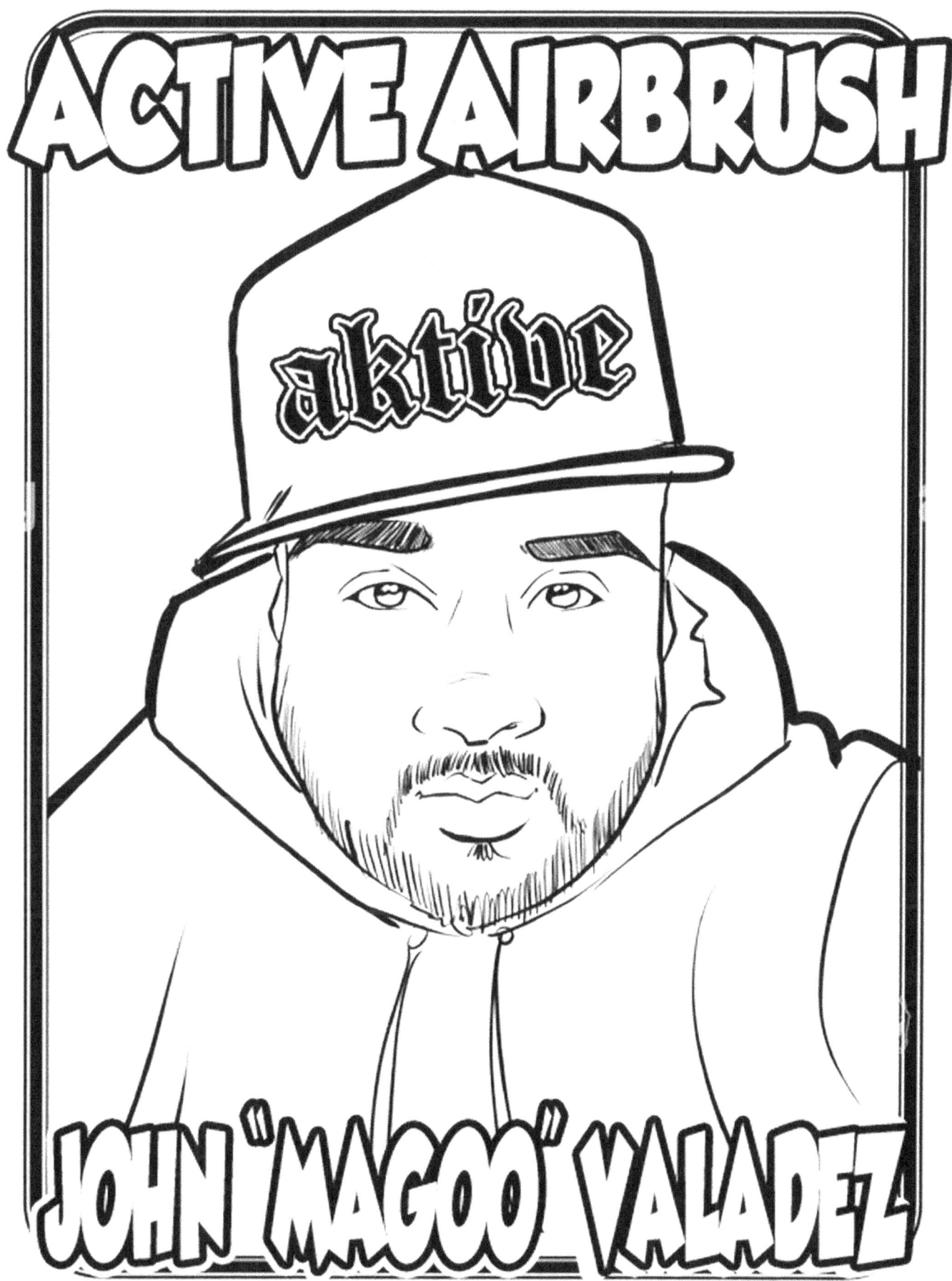

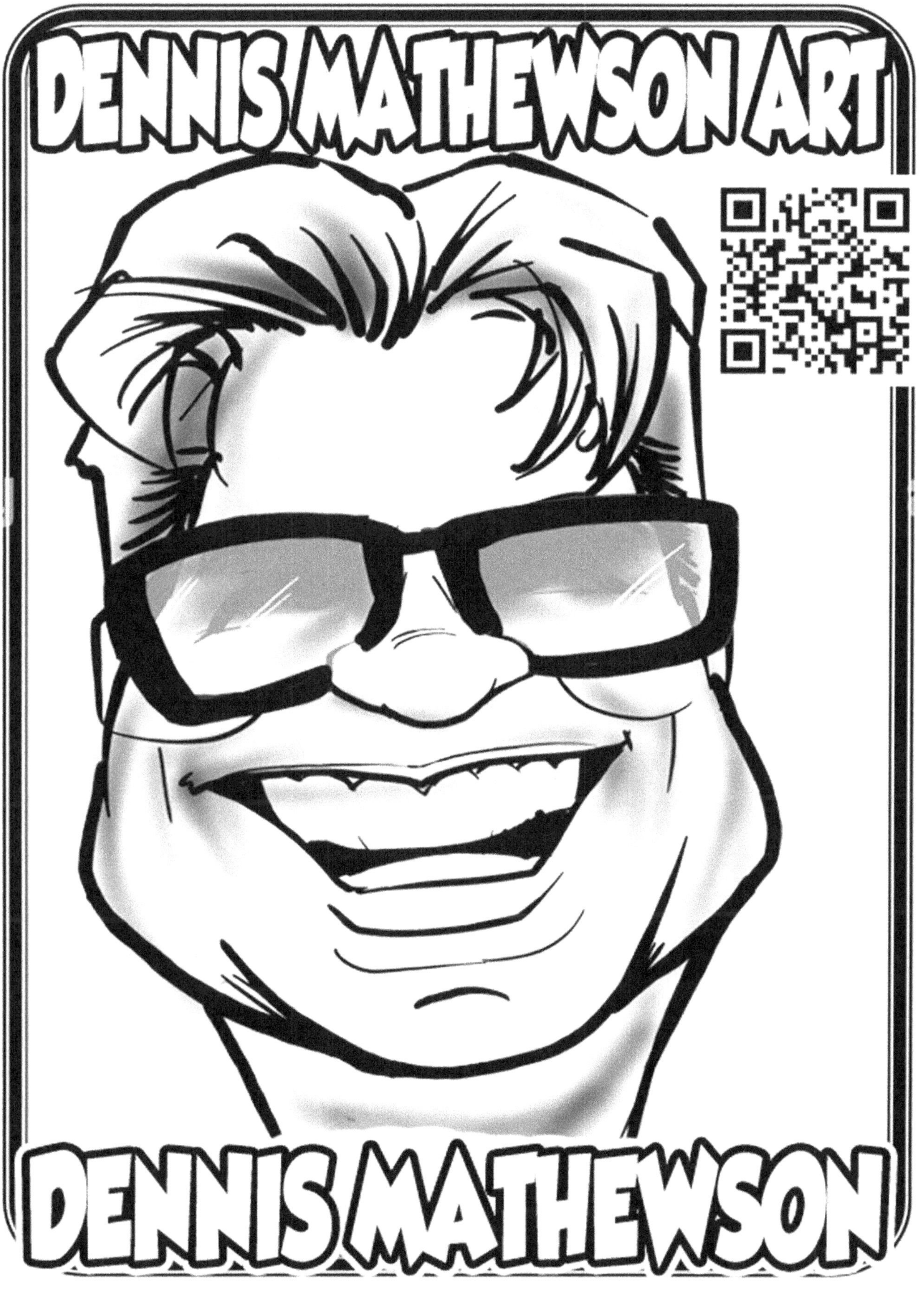
DENNIS MATHEWSON ART
DENNIS MATHEWSON

AIRGRAPHICS

SAM CLE' NEWTON

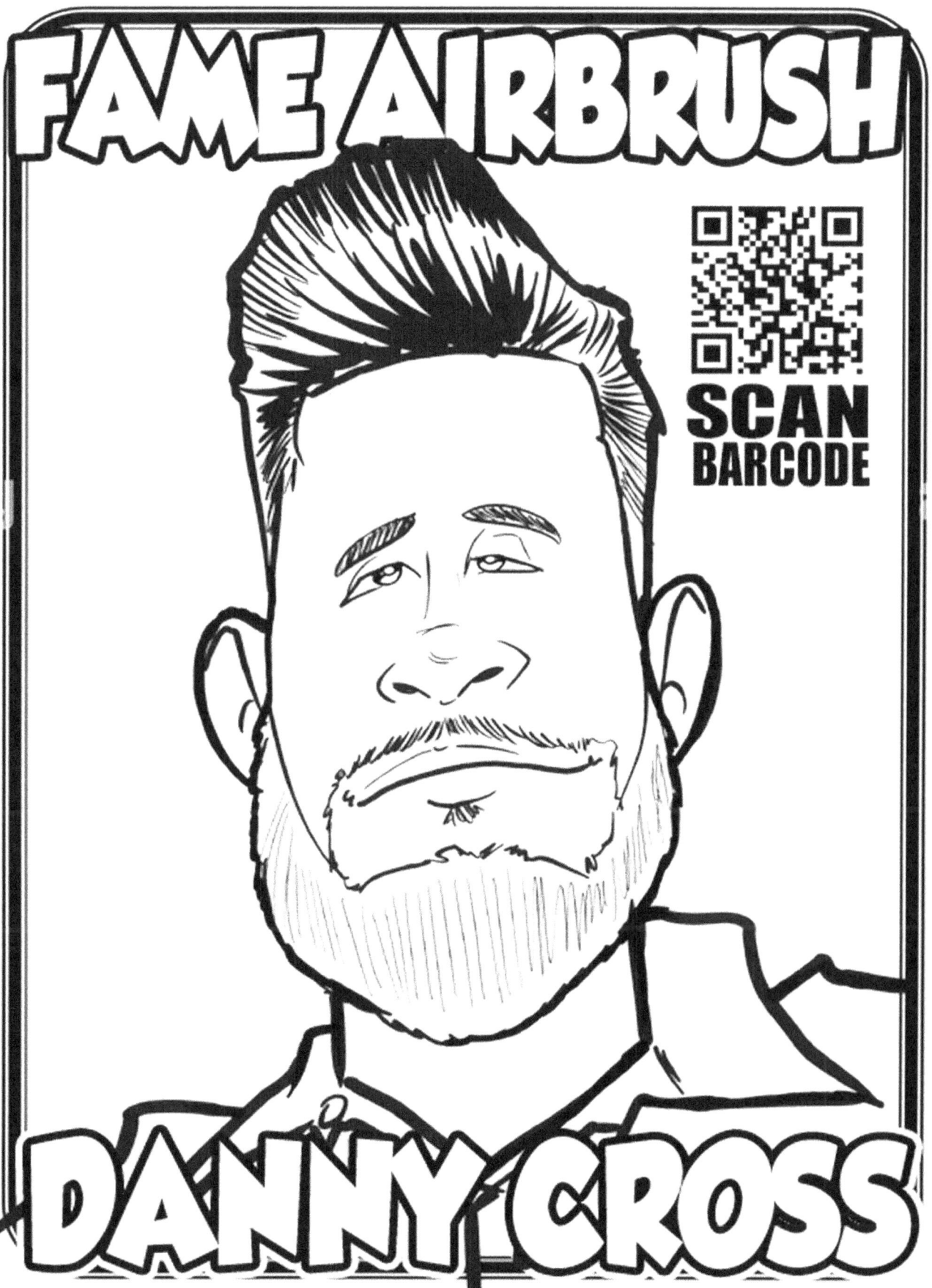

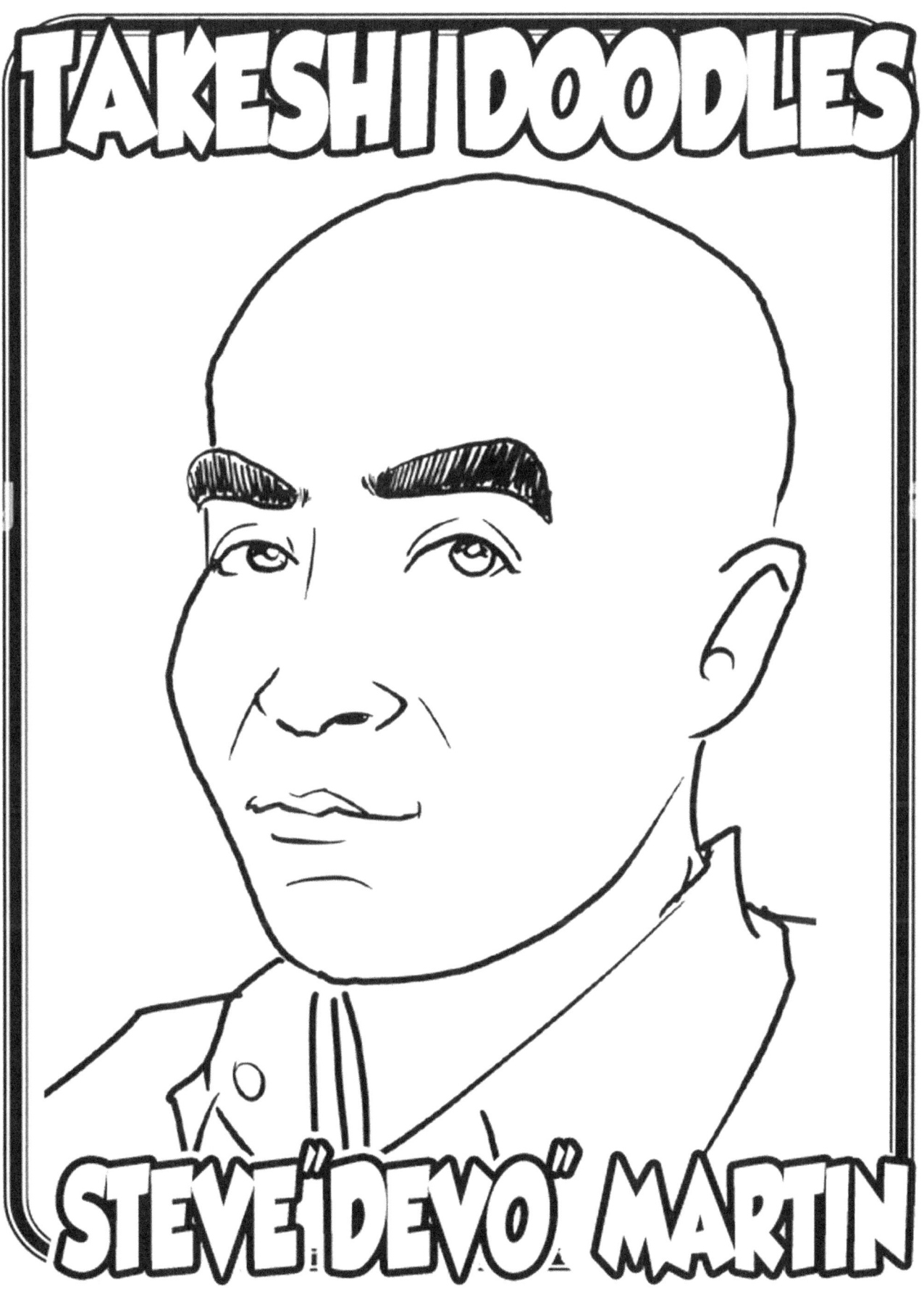

CUSTOM HOODLINERS

JEFF COPELAND

www.ingramcontent.com/pod-product-compliance
Lightning Source LLC
Chambersburg PA
CBHW082216290526
45794CB00009B/3566